Between Ball Games

Stories and Wisdom on
Raising Up and Cheering On
Strong Young Men

Amy Bloye

LEAFWOOD
P U B L I S H E R S
an imprint of Abilene Christian University Press

BETWEEN BALL GAMES
Stories and Wisdom on Raising Up and Cheering On Strong Young Men

Copyright © 2022 by Amy Bloye

ISBN 978-1-68426-391-2

Printed in the United States of America

Published in association with WordWise Media Services.

Library of Congress Cataloging-in-Publication Data

Names: Bloye, Amy, 1968– author.
Title: Between ball games : stories and wisdom on raising up and cheering on strong young men / Amy Bloye.
Description: Abilene, Texas : Leafwood Publishers, 2022.
Identifiers: LCCN 2021036945 (print) | LCCN 2021036946 (ebook) | ISBN 9781684263912 (paperback) | ISBN 9781684269358 (epub)
Subjects: LCSH: Mothers and sons. | Parenting. | Parents—Life skills guides. | Boys—Religious life. | Boys—Life skills guides.
Classification: LCC HQ755.85 .B59 2022 (print) | LCC HQ755.85 (ebook) | DDC 649.1/32—dc23
LC record available at https://lccn.loc.gov/2021036945
LC ebook record available at https://lccn.loc.gov/2021036946

Cover design by ThinkPen Design, LLC
Interior text design by Scribe Inc.
Sports icons designed by Rwdd_Studios / Freepik

Leafwood Publishers is an imprint of Abilene Christian University Press
ACU Box 29138
Abilene, Texas 79699
1-877-816-4455
www.leafwoodpublishers.com

22 23 24 25 26 27 / 7 6 5 4 3 2 1

To Brian, my partner in raising boys

Contents

Foreword

by Sue Ferguson

WHEN GOD MADE ME A MOM, HE LITERALLY GAVE ME THE DESIRE OF MY heart! Being Mom to my three kids—Amy, Josh, and Caleb—was my favorite job ever. And if I'm honest, the most challenging—and that's saying a lot because, like Amy Bloye, I taught junior high! I became a mom a bit later than many; all my closest friends had children before I did, and that gave me the opportunity to observe and take mental notes for when I got to join them on the adventure called parenting. A few of the big-picture things I learned watching others include the fact that this parenting thing is not for the weak. Second, there is not just one right way to navigate the parenting journey. And last, but certainly not least, having friends you trust to walk alongside you, reassuring you and cheering you on along the way, is essential! The insights, wisdom, and reassurance shared in *Between Ball Games* make Amy Bloye one of the women you will definitely want to put on your list of trusted cheerleaders.

Having taught junior high for nine years before having kids, and having a girl before my two boys were born, I learned that most boys are wired differently than most girls—the physicality of boys can be both exhausting and scary at times. After my son Josh broke his arm, I remember telling him that he could not ride his bike for six weeks. The next day while making my bed I heard a voice outside of my second-floor window, and there was Josh up the tree saying, "Hi, Mom!" I hadn't put climbing trees on the not-with-a-broken-arm list! At my daughter's birthday parties, the girls were busy and had fun, but no one got hurt, and the party ended with nothing broken. That was not the case at the boys' birthday parties—things were broken and boys were injured! We held many fun home birthday parties for my daughter, but I gained a new understanding of the Chuck E. Cheese birthday party craze after a couple of home parties for the boys. And don't even get me started on the tolerance I had to develop for stink and grossness—the things I found growing inside of duffel bags that had been tossed into a closet could have made for some great science projects! So if you are a mom of boys, I see you—I get it! And so does Amy Bloye.

In *Between Ball Games*, Amy tells it like it is. She opens her heart and shares a vast array of parenting experiences. Her authenticity and transparency about the daily struggles, the exhaustion, and the joy of raising her boys will have you laughing out loud in places and saying "Oh! It's not just me?" and "I can do this!" And Amy's wisdom and the lessons she learned on her parenting journey will provide you with both new ideas and the reassurance that you have what it takes to raise your boys. All along the way, she reminds us that God sees us, loves us and our kids, and will guide us as we help our kids become all that he has created them to be.

This book will become a road map for you as a boy mom and breathe hope into your heart. And be sure to share *Between Ball Games* with some fellow boy moms! Then find time to connect with those moms to discuss what has encouraged and challenged you to keep moving forward and to keep trusting God to guide you down the twisting road of raising boys. Amy even provides discussion questions you can use for these gatherings.

Remember, Mommas, there's only been one perfect child that ever walked this earth, and there have been no perfect earthly parents, and we aren't going to be the first. But with books like this, and with God's help, we can be moms who love, empower, and encourage our kids to follow that one perfect child, Jesus, as they journey through life.

Sue Ferguson
Associate Small Groups Director
Community Christian Church
Naperville, Illinois

But My Baby Dolls Were All Girls

WHEN I WAS A LITTLE GIRL PLAYING WITH DOLLS, I USED REAL DIAPERS and real baby clothes. I remember getting a toy baby stroller and play bottles. I cut my dolls' hair and stored their accessories in a purple trunk. My two favorite dolls I named Allison and Emily. They sat on my bed, and I nurtured them and cared for them. I was their little mother. I looked forward to the day when, at long last, I would have my own real-life babies. I would pick out matching hair bows and patent leather shoes. It never occurred to me, however, that my real-life babies would be boys! What? I never played boy mom. How did that even work?

Though I didn't play boy mom with my dolls, I now realize that God was developing a boy mom in me all along, an identity that would be my greatest challenge and the key that would open the most precious and unknown little compartment of my heart, the biggest source of joy and surprise, and a love that would be deeper and sweeter than anything I could have ever known: the indescribable love of a boy mom.

Do you know the story of Chinese bamboo? Once planted, the bamboo takes five years to show any sign of growth. It must be cultivated and watered for five full years without any apparent results, and then after being dormant for what seems like forever, the Chinese bamboo bursts from the ground. In as little as six weeks, the bamboo shoots to potentially eighty feet tall. The patience of the gardener reminds me of the gentle perseverance of those who are cultivating the growth of little boys. The long process of watering and waiting may seem daunting or make you feel unsure. The patience required to establish a strong root system is not for the faint of heart, but oh, just wait until those little sprigs of life begin to burst forth from that soil that you have been tending for all those years. Your contribution to what has taken place under the soil will return to you as you have been patiently investing in depth of character, goals, dreams, and a sure foundation that can withstand the storms of life. Do not be weary, dear gardener, for what you are doing right now is so important. Keep watering and waiting. You are developing strong men, and you have exactly what it takes.

CHAPTER ONE

You're Gonna Miss This

(Hold on to those sweet faces. Time is flying.)

NEW JEANS. NEW TENNIS SHOES. NEW SCHOOL YEAR. SCHOOL STARTS the first week of August in Georgia, and like a thief sneaking in to steal the last part of summertime, the early return to formal education had crept up on us again. I am most confident that not even parents are prepared to resume school duties that early! As we stood on the back deck in the crisp morning air, I watched my teenage boys reluctantly pose with sincere smiles for their obligatory first-day-of-school picture. We had checked off the list of school supplies, packed lunches, and prepared class schedules. I would wave bye as my boys pulled out of the driveway, no longer to be car riders with Mom. But first, the picture.

In the most random, unplanned, yet seemingly orchestrated eruption of their voices, my boys put their arms around each other and broke into a chorus that I will never forget: "You're gonna miss this. You're gonna want this back. You're gonna wish these days hadn't gone by so fast. These are some good times. So take a good look around. You may not know it now, but you're gonna miss this." The three of us had a moment. I tried to be cool and not let them see the big tears welling up in my eyes. Their impromptu country chorus had unexpectedly touched my hurried heart. I *would* miss this. The years of no first-day-of-school pictures were coming quickly, and I knew it. I could feel it hover nearby. And in some weird way, I wanted it, but I didn't. Could I have a little break but hold on to these sweet, fleeting days?

I have heard it said that the days are long and the years are short. Now I know that is a true statement because I have lived it and felt it and rushed it and savored it. Time has a way of disappearing. In fact, the clock has thrown a light on all that I thought I knew about parenting, and it all has to do with chilling out and relaxing and loving and spending precious time on things that really matter and not caring about what everyone thinks. If I could go back, I would yell less. I would sing and jump and play more. I would hold those little messy faces in my hands a moment longer.

I would see those strong-willed personalities as a foreshadowing of amazing strength and leadership and bold confidence. When I hoped my defiant toddlers would just *quit*, I wish I could have fast-forwarded twenty-plus years to see what it looks like to see them as young adults who *never* quit. If only I could have seen, when I wished I could break their stubborn wills, that they would have a stubborn motivation to succeed and win and fight for all things good.

I wish, when I faced challenging mornings and felt like a failure as a mom, that I could have seen into the future and glimpsed that God was doing his greatest work in my weakness, as the little boys I was raising would one day be men of strength and character. I would choose more often to see that God was in the very middle of making the most amazing men I have ever known.

Even in my exhaustion and frustration, I was blessed and thankful, but if I could, I would go back and remind myself of a few truths. I would anchor my thoughts in how lucky I was to be cleaning up messes and to be showing the love of Jesus and teaching his truth to tiny little humans who were listening to every word I said and who, one day, would make a difference. I would preach loudly to myself that I could do this difficult and rewarding mothering thing because so much was at stake and I was more equipped than I thought.

Sweet Mom, you have been given every single thing that you need to raise this boy. You have got this, and you are not alone. In the profound need of your heart to know that you are a good mother and that you are doing a good job, God swoops in with a resounding *yes!* He will give you everything you need only one day at a time. Spend zero minutes in self-doubt and regret. Get up, love big, and trust that you are adding one drop of amazing to every day.

> *"I am with you, mighty warrior." (Judges 6:12)*

Raising boys is such a unique adventure! They are such interesting creatures that often take the form of messy hair, sweaty bodies, and interesting smells. Don't let the exterior fool you. Inside every boy is a yearning heart that needs his mom to demonstrate the unique balance of strength and tenderness, how to love others well and be true to the man God has called him to be. Don't be thrown when one day you hug your son and feel man-shoulders within your arms. Your role may be shifting from mom to coach to friend, but your son will always need his mom.

—Sherry Surratt, executive director of
parent strategy for Orange, former
CEO of Mothers of Preschoolers

CHAPTER TWO

Jumbo Ketchup Bottles

(Your son is a little warrior. Who cares if he spills the ketchup?)

THERE HE WAS, ON HIS KNEES ON THE CHAIR AT THE KITCHEN TABLE. My youngest male offspring wrestled with the jumbo ketchup bottle like it was his job. His face was strained and his arm hooked around the bottle, taming it yet shaking it to produce the desired amount of the condiment. I was a fan of the wholesale club jumbo grocery items. They are great money savers if your child has the ability to lift them. I sat observing at the other end of the table. "Brian, grab that ketchup! Zach is getting ready to spill it everywhere!" I ordered. What happened next irritated me yet changed my parenting forever.

Brian looked knowingly at my boys and then back at me. The glance informed me that I was not in the club. Two boys and their dad had an understanding, and I was on the outs. A woman in a house with three men. "Oh, that's my boy, and he is a warrior!" Brian exclaimed. "Well, your little warrior is about to make a huge mess!" I contended. I do not remember what we ate that night, but I remember how I felt. I was doing my best to control all the things. I had wanted everyone to be neat and tidy and . . . girly, I suppose.

When Brian suggested at the dinner table that I read *Wild at Heart* by John Eldredge, I am pretty sure I royally rolled my eyes. I knew all about boys. I was raising two of them and doing a dang good job. The problem was this: I was a girl. I didn't have the heart of a man, and so I needed to be educated on the subject.

My book arrived in a timely manner, and I grudgingly began to read. I read about the question that, from the beginning of time, every single living male has in his heart—a question that has been strategically placed there by the hand of God. I learned that each old man, teenage boy, and male child has a heart that poses a question to be answered. The question is this: Do I have what it takes? Now, ultimately only God can answer life's biggest question of the heart, but it is our honor and privilege to point our boys toward that answer every day. For the answer from God and from us is a resounding yes! Each night, before the boys went to sleep, Brian would look them in the eyes and say, "You have got what it takes." Even now, I hear him reassure them of that truth over and over again. Women and girls also want to know if we have what it takes, but that is not the nagging question of our hearts. (We have another question, by the way.) And you must read Eldredge's wife Stasi's book *Captivating*, which also changed my life, and I very rarely use the phrase "changed my life." I address this question in chapter 32.

The book poured over me and informed me like a soothing oil. Had my thinking not been rescued by the ketchup bottle incident, I would have remained ignorant of this matter and so many more about the heart of a man. Moms, please learn what you can about the heart that beats inside of your son; it is so very different from your own.

To accede to Brian's warrior label, I am learning (it is a lifelong process, girls) that men are indeed created to be warriors. They are intricately designed to be strong and confident and to protect. To force it to be delicate or soft will ruin a male spirit, and I fear that many women are guilty of unknowingly softening and trying to tame the man, who is supposed to be wild and free. The heart of a man is so unique and valuable. Why would we want to feminize it?

Perhaps we tell ourselves that it is easier to keep a man calm rather than deal with his messiness. He is gritty and rough edged. The God-man, Jesus, was also fierce. The Bible refers to him as a lion, beautiful and strong, having the ability to protect and lead. Somehow the humanity in motherhood questions whether we can handle the strength of a boy, a man. Could it be that we fear losing control, so we attempt to make them like us?

James Dobson, in his book *Bringing Up Boys*, refers to mothers that tell boys that they cannot play with toy guns. He says that if you take all their guns away, they will chew their bologna into the shape of a gun![1] I am certain that in our desire to control, we must allow them to be boys. We can do just that, release them to be masculine, but we, as women, cannot impart masculinity to a boy. Only a man can do that. We cannot teach them to be men. If your son does not have a solid role model in his life, it is important that you find opportunities for him to be around men that will, by their very existence, teach your son the role of manhood.

Teaching third grade was a window of knowledge for me about how boys and girls learn. It is unfortunate that so many boys, who learn by actively doing, are made to sit in neat rows and do worksheets. I recall teachers threatening to take away recess from those squirmy little guys, and I learned early on that recess was my friend. The teachers who withheld it only hurt themselves, as those boys desperately needed to run and play! The girls might stand and talk around the swing sets, but the boys sweated profusely. Everyone was better because of recess. I am a big fan! And I remember the boys in my class brought in their homemade jerseys, names and numbers written on T-shirts with markers. Recess was real in my class, and we played hard. Just thinking about it makes me smile. Do you remember the little air sounds that boys make when they put their hands under their armpits and move their arms like a flying wing? What is it about gassy sounds that make little boys die laughing? One little third-grade boy decided that it would be fun to make those sounds in my classroom. Each time I turned around and wrote on the board, I heard another arm squeak. Instead of scolding and bemoaning the sounds, I decided that everyone should participate! All the little winged warriors in the class stood with permission and squeaked their arms to their greatest delight. I have not often seen such utter amusement and thrill in the classroom as the day the boys were released to revel in their flapping wings. Some stood on their chairs, heads thrown back in laughter. It was the greatest display of juvenile maleness, and each and every girl looked on in total bewilderment. A true contrast. The miniature men were pleased, and we could move on with our lesson. It was probably the best two-minute decision I made in teaching!

I will close with one last story. I read about a leader whose parents sent him across the world by himself as a preteen. He traveled with an itinerary and a passport. Decades ago, before social media or the internet, he had to pioneer on his own to find his way to his next destination, secure transportation, and manage his money. His parents were willing to give him huge responsibilities at a young age—not overprotect but rather take risks—in their assumption that he would grow and be a leader of leaders. Now, I am not suggesting that we throw our children on boats and planes and send them to lands unknown. I am, however, challenged to help our boys do difficult things. Some mothers won't let their son carry his own McDonald's tray for fear that he may drop it. What if he does drop it? Who cares? He will pick it up and learn how to carry it like a beast. If he spills the jumbo ketchup bottle and makes a huge mess, who cares? I would rather clean up a mess than communicate to my son that I don't believe he is strong enough to squirt some ketchup on his own burger.

Your son may be technologically brilliant, an artist, or a musician. He may not love hunting or fishing, yet his heart is masculine and strong. Moms, dads, let's think big. Let's help our young warriors to be strong, capable men who actually think that they can do anything. God has put a question in their hearts. Do they have what it takes? Although we are not the ones who even have the ability to fully answer their question, we are meant to point them powerfully to the One who can. Yes, because of Jesus they have exactly what it takes! They are made to be and do something great, and we get the honor of helping them realize it.

> *The Lord is a warrior. (Exodus 15:3 NLT)*

Here is this man, brave, strong, standing tall above me, and with a beard! My little boy is a man! I am so proud that he is the one who breaches the doorway to defend the weak, the one who runs toward danger to keep everyone else safe. I watched him grow up wanting to be the good guy, the hero, the one who saves the day. He is that hero. He is a police officer. The prayers for this man—once my little, tiny guy—remain the same steadfast requests of the Lord: Please, Jesus, please keep my boy safe. Keep him healthy and make him strong. Keep him in the very center of your will. Surround him with you and make him a mighty man that God can use. I know this: God has answered that prayer many times, and I will continue on my knees talking to Jesus on his behalf, because my boy—the tall, brave man—will never be safer than he is when he is doing what God has called him to do.

—Dr. Kathryn Miller, Liberty University
School of Nursing

CHAPTER THREE

We Got an A on Our Gorilla Science Project

(Love big and help each other.)

YOU CAN FIND THE COOLEST, MOST RANDOM STUFF AT GOODWILL. AS I visually scanned the shelves in the back of our local thrift store, I found a little treasure, one that confirmed to me that my (our) science project was going to rock. Fluffed in a pile on a shelf was a fabric of sorts, a furry material that had a chunk cut out of it. It looked like a big stuffed animal wannabe. Somewhere, someone legitimately thought that this cut-up, hideous piece was actually desirable. Who, pray tell, would ever in the history of thrifty finds think that this was something they wanted to actually purchase? Evidently, I did. This piece practically willed itself to me when my desperation as a mother of a middle school boy with a science project must have been almost tangibly obvious.

"We" must have waited until the very last minute to even announce that "we" had a project due in, most likely, the next twenty-three hours. Now, Zach was scattered, as most middle school boys can be, and he was active and funny, but one thing he was not was content to do less than his very best. He would, at the last minute, crank out an A each and every time. Procrastination fueled him, and his high standards required an all-out effort. Because he was managing many more projects and papers and sports and church and, I am going to guess, some kind of cast or sling, I found this project to be an area that I could step into. I could help—and by help, I mean Brian and I could stay up until midnight and create a gorilla out of this furry thrift store find. It was now a goal, a race against time. Dang, it was my project, and it was going to be awesome!

Digging through assorted boxes in our basement, I found an old stuffed animal snake with crazy big eyes. He had not been upstairs in a bit, and all I saw in that discarded toy was a pair of gorilla eyes. Brian broke out a glue gun like it was his job, and I designed red lips of felt. A gorilla nose morphed into being as Brian crafted a piece of fake leather from my old purse. He made that nose with an enthusiasm unknown to mankind. Our gorilla was a mask with a handheld stick (a paint stirring stick from Home Depot) that Zach would hold over his face while he read his paper to the class. As we designed our primate and Zach typed the last of his report, we realized that he had to get up early for Fellowship of Christian Athletes, so he reluctantly, and with much gratitude, climbed the stairs to bed. Brian and I promised we were almost finished and assured him that he should get some sleep. When the clock told us we too needed to retire, we finished our gorilla, and I promise you, it was a boastful piece. We were more than content with our accomplishment, but the next week, when we got an A, the pleasure was all ours.

There is a healthy balance between helping our kids and doing too much to enable them. I have great respect for parents who develop independence in their kids at an early age; they do not comply with last-minute requests due to a lack of planning. These moms want their kid to be fully emotionally and financially mature and independent, and they will be as firm or as steadfast as they need to be in order to ensure that their child develops a sense of maturity and self-discipline early on.

On the other hand, there are parents who want their child to like them and be their friend, so they will do anything and everything to ensure that the child is pleased. I have seen well-meaning parents who, in my opinion, are actually scared of their child. Scared their child will disapprove or act out. They fear they will lose their friendship.

If only our little ones were born with a manual on how to raise them, right? I am finding that in the search for the correct parenting style, many factors contribute to the way we choose to interact with our children.

If your parents were overly strict or lavishly lenient with you, you may choose to be the opposite, or you may not be able to help yourself, and you may unknowingly mirror their behavior. So much of the way we parent stems from our own upbringing. If you had very little growing up, you may want to give your children all the things you never had. Maybe your own parents were free spirits and had lots of kids and animals and emotions were big and hugs were frequent. However your past was painted, it has shaped you, and that fact itself is worth considering.

Your personality, your strengths and weaknesses, your giftedness, your available resources, and the environment in which you raise your children all contribute to your journey as parents. I have friends whose children have situations that also contribute to the ways they are parented: children with special needs, sons and daughters who have been bullied, kids who have been uprooted or have dealt with loss, injury, or divorce. Each requires special attention and a willingness to adapt your preferred, preplanned parenting style.

There have been times when I have felt like I just got things figured out, and behold, everything changed. Furthermore, what you may consider to be a successful tactic with one child may, in fact, not work the same way with another one. No two are exactly alike, and cookie-cutter parenting may not always be the answer.

So should we do the gorilla project or not?

I will tell you about Max Mills. My parents moved us from South Florida to northern Indiana when I was in the ninth grade. I went from private school to public school. Hot and humid sunny days to snowplows and moon boots. From the beach to the soybean field. I went from having lots of friends to having to make all new friends. Amid all the change in my life as a young teenager, a beautiful castle is vividly etched in my mind. The castle pillars were toilet paper rolls covered in the most spectacular spackling compound. Its rigid texture was composed of the watered-down compound precisely dripped in lovely heaps. Blue food coloring stained the rippled moat that lay under the carefully constructed drawbridge. No finer castle ever saw the halls of Warsaw High School.

We had moved to Indiana for my dad to go back to school and get his master's degree, so Dad and I were both in school together. Dad was a perfect student and graduated magna cum laude with all As. He studied and worked more than full time. (I actually learned to study from watching my dad draw word pictures on poster paper and tape them to the dining room walls during his exam week.) To say that Dad was busy is an understatement, so when he cut a huge board and went to the store and purchased our castle supplies, when he labored on my miniature medieval replica, I caught something. It was not taught, but I caught it.

I caught how to make someone feel like they are valuable and worthy. I soaked in what it feels like to be busy but to have someone who is busier stop and speak loudly into your life with their actions. Sure, I could have made a forgettable nominal project on my very own and been independent and self-sufficient in Mrs. White's honors World Literature class, but something more happened. Something was instilled in me, and today I am writing about it.

I decided somewhere in my subconscious self that I wanted to be like Dad, who chose to stay and get a second master's degree, because it was my senior year, and he and Mom did not want me to have to move again during my last year in high school. I wanted to powerfully speak into the lives of my children like that with a yes. Yes, I will bring your forgotten lunch to school. Yes, I will make an extra trip to the store to get you exactly what you need. Yes, I will be inconvenienced and probably risk high esteem from my more proper and precise peers. I will say yes, and I will have sense enough to know when to help my boys cultivate their own independence and growth.

I guess it just thrills me to make their lives sweeter. If I can make my boys' lives better for one single day, then I am going to do whatever it takes until I am an old, old lady with blue hair and false teeth. Then I will still be up in their business, loving them with all my geriatric, Enneagram-type-two heart. No one has ever been encouraged too much. We are all in, Brian Bloye and I. We want to say it and buy it and help with it and cheer for it and go to it and dream about it and support it with all the prayers.

So make the dang gorilla.

Don't regret it; life is short.

Love big!

> *Keep each other's spirits up so that no one falls behind or drops out. (Ephesians 6:18 MSG)*

CHAPTER FOUR

I Should Have Been an Orthopedic Doctor!

(Dealing with energy and injury.)

AT ONE POINT, OUR CLOSET BOASTED AN ABSURD AMOUNT OF WOUND care, knee wraps, and kinesiology tape and a wide array of crutches, slings, and splints. I would eventually (in the case of a very unalarming and most likely illegitimate minor injury) point, in fact, in the general direction of these products: "There. Dig through the ancient wraps our insurance once partially purchased, and see if you might find relief for your most recent ailment!"

For the leg injuries, "Try to run," we said.

For many other mishaps, "Maybe it's not broken," we hoped.

Epsom salts were our friend. Our freezer, the keeper of our many ice packs.

Having never broken a bone, I had no anticipation of becoming friends with the talented urgent care professionals near our house. Who knew we would be seeing so much of each other? We were there much too often.

At a very young age, Taylor brought boundless energy—and a laundry list of injuries. In total, he broke eleven bones: collarbone, leg, two back bones, hand, wrist, finger, arm, same hand again, the other hand, another finger, and a thumb. He had a slipped disc, stitches in his mouth, and a couple MRIs.

Zach sported a festive green "Christmas cast" at the age of two and followed up with a sprained MCL, three dislocated elbows, another broken arm, stitches in his head and arm, a torn ligament in his thumb, several MRIs, a sport-ending back injury, and labrum surgery. These do not include the often more traumatic trips to the ER where the diagnosis was less serious. Yes, boys may be quite active, energetic, and injury prone.

I recall one mother commenting, "You just seem so chilled out while your boys are jumping off the top of the bleachers." I am fairly certain that my nerves were so shot that I had no energy left to worry. If you did not grow up with boys, you may be surprised at the infinite supply of energy most of them have. Their thirst for adventure may supersede all common sense.

As mothers, we may live in fear of what could happen. And sure enough, these calamities hit because we live in a fallen world, and for that reason, we should be cautious and instill safety measures as we instruct our boys.

Moms, there is a difference between being cautious and wise and being overly protective and fearful. If you are wise, you can impart wisdom to your son, but if you regularly overreact in fear, you will teach your son to live in fear as well. Protect, but don't overprotect. We must pray specifically and give our worries to God, who cares more for our boys than we possibly can. After that, we have to remind ourselves that these little men (or big men) are ours on loan to love and nurture, and we must teach them to eventually entrust their own worries to God.

As Smalls's mother said in the movie *The Sandlot*, "Climb trees! Hop fences. Get into trouble."

> *Cast all your care upon him, for he cares for you. (1 Peter 5:7)*

Having a solid and healthy relationship with my stepson is something I have cared deeply about, but like most stepmom things, it didn't happen overnight. As I got to know him more and more, I realized how much he and I actually have in common. Cultivating little moments around those common threads created a fun and special bond that we have to this day. As our relationship grew, I found that I really could have a voice in his life. The further our relationship developed, the more I realized that I could be one more voice encouraging him, believing in him, speaking truth to him, not replacing the already special relationship he has with his mom, but being one more person who has the opportunity to breathe life and truth into him—what a gift!

—Christie Meldrim, stepmom

CHAPTER FIVE

Spit It Out

(Talking to your boys without driving them crazy.)

THE DOORBELL RANG, AND WE SCURRIED EXPECTANTLY TO OPEN THE door. It was Brian's dad; he had a happy grin as he greeted Brian and me with his two sidekicks. Our little boys tightly held their dollar store prizes in one hand and their McDonald's treats in the other. Sipping on their straws, they beamed sheepishly. Grandpa was not supposed to take them to get treasures. This was supposed to be an outing where he talked some sense into them and told them to stop fighting and to respect their parents. How could I rebuke him? He had saved the day. "Oh, they can hear much better when they are eating McDonald's," he said. "We have an agreement." He confirmed their promise of good behavior in the future. Gosh, I miss that man. When the boys were six and nine, he passed away in a rafting accident. He was one of our greatest heroes, and we get choked up just thinking about the large part of their lives that he has missed out on. Many times he spoke sweet words of encouragement and admonished our boys to be great men. Many times he took them to the toy store. We could have used his advice a lot these past sixteen years. He himself was a treasure. Sometimes you talk to your boys and you just can't get through to them, and you need to enlist a little help. Sometimes we have talked enough, and sometimes we still ask ourselves, "What would your dad do?"

Moms, I am going to say it straight up. There are times that we frustrate our boys with our words. Are you ever the recipient of glazed-over stares? My boys have said many times, "OK, I've got it, Mom." I know I have exasperated them with my word count. I know better, and I have worked very specifically in my house of men to summarize and think before I speak, but still, I sometimes go over my welcome words, especially with advice or instructions.

How can we communicate clearly to our boys without frustrating them?

Say It Once. We do not need to keep repeating the instructions or retelling the same thing we just said. Often, I repeat myself because I do not think they are listening. Guys, can you give us an "OK" or a sign that you caught it? Then we can stop rambling. Maybe we can establish a plan for eye contact or a positive response so we will know that you heard and can stop talking.

Do Not Give Too Many Details. Give the shortened version of the story and get to the point. In fact, my boys have mentioned that it is helpful to state the bottom line upfront and then explain it instead of giving all the details and making them wonder what the point is. We girls enjoy the detailed pathway, anticipating the ending, but the boys usually want the key point first.

Use a Normal Voice. Squeaky, baby, or condescending tones do not serve us well. In my attempts to not lose my cool, I have adopted a singsongy, overly kind, smiley voice that says, "I am really mad, but I am trying not to bite your head off." Hear yourself and stop. Use your normal, kind voice.

One of the best ways to open lines of communication is to ask questions. Questions bring about a dialogue between two people and may generate more obedient results than barking commands. Listen attentively when they are talking and inquire with phrases like "It sounds like you are saying . . . ," "How did that make you feel?" or "I am understanding that . . ."

Ask God for Wisdom. James 1:5 tells us that if we lack wisdom, we should ask God for it, and he will give it. Do not drift into mindless chatter or rebuke; instead, ask for wisdom before you have an important conversation, and God will give it to you. He says that he will not even make you feel ridiculous for asking, and he will not just give you a tiny bit of it. He will pour wisdom out on you if you will only ask.

Vent to Jesus. Often, I catch myself venting out loud in worry or complaint. When my moment of rant is over, I think to myself, "Is that really what I wanted to say with the little time I have been given with my boys today?" It doesn't usually come out and land the way I had hoped. I may wish that I could reel it back in and start over. I am learning to vent my frustrations and less attractive moody complaints to God and use my few times of influence with my young men in more pleasant conversation.

Ask for One Minute. I like to ask, "Could I have one minute of your time? I want to share something with you." Usually they will stop and listen if they know I am consciously aware of a time limit.

"Lighten Up." Jen Hatmaker says this in her book *For the Love*. I could not agree more. She continues, "We cannot prickle over every little thing. Learn to hold the biting remark, the wounded reaction, the irritated retort.... Everything cannot be a big deal, because when the big deals actually happen, we're too worn-out to handle them."[1]

Do Not Be One of "Those" Mothers. My son is a coach at a large high school, and on the weekends, he coaches a traveling baseball team of eighteen-year-olds. I know firsthand that there are loud, obnoxious mothers who compromise their boys' futures with their abundance of unbridled words. Always speak with grace.

The Child Development Institute has some brilliant advice on their website. These are great nuggets of insight:

- "Use your child's name. Your own name is music to your ears. Our kids are no different, and it helps to get their attention before delivering your message. E.g., 'George, please go and get....' Young children can often only concentrate on one thing at a time. Call your child's name until you have their attention before you speak."

- "Suggest options and alternatives. When you want your kids to cooperate with you, it is far easier if they can understand why they need to do something and how it is to their advantage to do so. They need to see the importance of following our directions. For example: 'When you get dressed, you may go outside with Daddy.' 'Which book would you like to read, this one or that one?' 'When you get dressed for school, you may then play with your toys.' Adopting words like 'when' and 'which' makes the child feel as though they have choices, even though there is no room for negotiation. Using these words works far better than using 'if' words."

- "Explain what you want with 'I' messages. When asking your child to do something, you will receive a greater response by explaining what you want regarding thoughts and feelings by using 'I messages.' This is far more effective than using orders or 'you messages.' It lets your child know how their behavior makes you feel. Kids sometimes don't consider how their behavior will affect others. By using this strategy, it may help to give more considerations to their actions, and it gives them more responsibility to change their behavior. For example, 'I would like you to come over here, please,' instead of 'Come over here,' or 'I would like you to give Oliver a turn please,' instead of 'Give Oliver a turn!' It is a softer approach and children who wish to please others will respond to this type of language. Explaining how you feel also helps kids to see why they should comply. For example, 'When you run away from Mommy in the store, I feel worried because you could get lost.' Use 'when you . . . I feel . . . because . . .' words."

- "Give notice. If your child is fully engrossed in an activity and it is time to leave, give them notice, so they get used to the idea. For example, 'George, it is nearly time to go. Start saying goodbye to the puppy please.'"

- "Don't interrupt. Try not to interrupt or scold your kids when they are telling you a story. Kids will lose interest in sharing their feelings with you if you shift away from their story and use the time to teach them a lesson. . . . Listening is just as important as talking."[2]

Our words have the power to push our boys away or draw them in. What a privilege we have as parents to be the ones whose words beckon them into a deeper relationship. You may have to tag-team a trip to McDonald's with grandpa or a dollar store prize, but don't give up. Although it may take a village to help us out, words of life are ours to distribute.

> *Even fools are thought wise when they keep silent; with their mouths shut, they seem intelligent. (Proverbs 17:28 NLT)*

"Let them go." As I sat there crying, these were the words I heard at my son's college orientation. I realized his whole life had been a journey of different milestones where I learned to let him go and supported him along the way. Sometimes our fears and our own needs cause us to hold tight instead of allowing them to spread their wings, but it's important to encourage their manhood and freedom at different moments as they grow up. Champion their leadership, speak life into the man they can become, and help encourage them when they get it wrong.

—Danielle Newsome

CHAPTER SIX

I Left My Boy on Top of a Mountain

(When you realize they were actually listening.)

THE MOUNTAIN WAS CURVY AND STEEP, AND THE TIRES OF TAYLOR'S truck seemed to climb with an understanding that the mountain underneath was to become a familiar trail for the next four years. Taking your son to college is an emotional surprise. Lots of excitement coupled with a little grief, an era ended, and a new road ahead for all of us. *Have I done enough?* I asked myself. *Have I taught diligently enough? Have our family values been instilled in this child, now a man? Will he call? Will he ever need me again?*

As the truck continued to climb, I kept my eyes ahead. I have always been afraid of heights, and the narrow drop-offs seemed to personify all the scary things that leaving my son on a mountain could possibly imply. I began to ramble my last-ditch effort at motherly instruction. "Be careful driving on this mountain. It is dangerous, you know! And those other kids, the other drivers, those are the ones I am really concerned about." I was politely interrupted, and in the sweetest way he assured me, "Mom, your speeches ring continuously in my ears." I'm sure he was saying "Be quiet" in a nice way, but somehow, I felt comforted and relieved that not all my speeches had gone unheard. He would be OK.

Alas, I am not the only parent giving advice. The parent-king in Proverbs 4:23 employs the following: "Take hold of my instructions; don't let them go. Guard them, for they are the key to life.... My child, pay attention to what I say. Listen carefully to my words.... Guard your heart above all else, for it determines the course of your life."

We all want to know if they remember anything we said. Will they remember what we told them when they were busy acting as though they were not listening? Will our words make a difference in the decisions they make? I want to tell you yes. I believe they hear us, and I have been encouraged to see firsthand that they were actually listening.

Taylor, since graduating from college, has played independent professional baseball in four different cities for the past several years. Each city has been lovely for us to explore. He has played in California, Illinois, and North Dakota and Sydney, Australia. Each opportunity has been unique, and the people he has encountered have been unforgettable. We were able to visit the stateside cities each spring, but when we were not there, we watched at home online. The announcers and mascots and the interactive, crowd-pleasing competitions are unique to the minor league feel of small-town professional baseball. The fans are great, and the players are all heart and soul. You can practically smell the concessions through the screen in your living room a thousand miles away.

The thing that has been even more exciting than watching my son pitch in the game that he loves in a packed, beautiful stadium is hearing about his conversations after the games. Each season has been characterized by one or two people who have been seemingly placed in Taylor's life for a purpose. Each one has had a need, and Taylor has been there to help and point each of these specific friends to truth and to Jesus. Often we ask him for updates about living on the road and traveling many miles to games in other states. We hear stories of bus trips and competitive rivalries, but when he tells us about the investment he is making in the lives of people and when he shares that this unique athletic opportunity is more about people than it is about a game, I know he gets it. I can see that as a young person, he was listening.

Do you ever hear your children copy your words when they are talking to their friends? When my boys were little, I would hear them playing and I would catch a phrase of my own that they were repeating. "That sounds like me!" I realized. You learn quickly that they will say the same good or bad things that you say when they are little. It is similar when they are grown.

Our kids not only hear what we say, but they watch what we do, and certainly, it has been confirmed that our actions are louder than our words. I had a teacher in college whose words impacted me, but the picture I recall in my mind of her pushing and pulling school desks out of line and moving them into groups has affected me even more than her words. Dr. Carwile taught us that kids learn best when they are experiencing something and not stuck looking forward in a row. As she pulled the desks out of rows to make her point, she reminded us of the verse at the top of her syllabus (Phil. 4:9 NLT): "Keep putting into practice all you learned and received from me—everything you heard from me and saw me doing. Then the God of peace will be with you." It is not just our words or lessons and speeches that our boys will remember. Our actions are etched more deeply in their minds.

When they see you calm in the midst of chaos, when they feel your love and assurance, when they see you serving your family and honoring your husband, when they see you reading your Bible and taking food to someone in need or working diligently to complete a work project, you are speaking loudly.

When your son stands up for what is right, when he serves or gives good advice, when he helps with the dishes or values family, you will know he was listening. All the hours and years that you pour into those little guys somehow seem to rush in and confirm that you did the best you could do, and it was enough.

Mom, I just want to encourage you today. You give up a lot, and you instinctively want your son to be a good man. Fast-forward to the day he is grown and can thank you for all the advice you have given him. But for now, do not worry. Just do what you can do today and deposit little lessons into his heart, and he will remember.

> *Instruct the wise and they will be even wiser. Teach the righteous, and they will learn even more. (Proverbs 9:9 NLT)*

Ideally, as grandparents, our homes, our hugs, are extensions of the safe, loving homes that our grandchildren are growing up in. Ideally, we are reinforcements, coming alongside our children, cheering them on, cheering our grandchildren on. But often life takes a turn, and we are called to grandparent in a less than ideal setting. We are to pray earnestly, listen more, and love big. It is here, in these times, that it is so vital that our grandbabies know that our love for them is unconditional, that we will listen to their little voices, and that we are on their team. Continually seeking God's guidance in how we do this and praying fervently for our children to be led by him are essential components to navigating this new, layered, and challenging journey ahead.

—Donna Robbins, a.k.a. Gigi, creator
@unsophisticatedgirl

CHAPTER SEVEN

Buy Yourself a Pink Towel

(Remembering to care for yourself.)

AS I AM WRITING THIS CHAPTER, I AM IN AN AIRPLANE, FLYING FROM Atlanta to Montana to pick up my new eight-week-old puppy and bring her home. Lucy Montana is my dream dog of sorts. I have not met her, but I picked her out of sixteen puppies based on the fact that she is a chocolate doodle, a dog I have wanted for many years. My friend Jen is flying with me. She is a flight attendant, and she got me on the plane with a buddy pass. She is truly that—a buddy and a treasure. We decided to make a day out of it, and so we plan to shop and eat something fabulous, snag my dog, and fly home.

I have not always been so kind to myself. When Brian and I were newly married, before the boys were born, we were in student ministry in a very large church. Brian was a pastor of middle school students and later to high school students. As you can imagine, we had a very active and rewarding life, and we were never home. Our church had some pretty cool and talented high school kids, and we had teams that would perform in detention homes and even abroad. I went with our teams to Russia when I was one month pregnant and generally sick. Yes, I did. On this trip, we had a twenty-four-hour bus ride from Moscow to Ukraine. Our students did gymnastics, martial arts, skateboarding and biking, singing, and drama.

In addition to teams, we had an event basically every weekend. Certainly, church three times a week was normal then. Add to that all-nighters and amusement park trips, snow camp, bonfires, and gym nights. It was honestly overwhelming. I had my own job, so after I taught school all week, I helped Brian all weekend.

One night when we rolled in late from another event, I literally collapsed in Brian's arms, and we fell back on the couch. "I just don't think I can keep going at this pace. I can't do this anymore," I admitted. After that night, we began to reevaluate our hectic schedule. We were doing wonderful things, but we never took a break. I often refer to that night when I was, as I call it, "at the end of my rope," and we recall together how we do not want to arrive at that place again.

Consider this, my busy friend: even God took a break. Not that he needed one. I love how author and pastor Tony Evans points out how God was not all sweaty and tired from the work of creation, yet even though he did not need rest, he modeled it for us. God created the whole world in six days, and on the seventh day, he rested. He chose to act in a manner of rejuvenation, rhythm, rest, and even reflection (He looked at his creation and said it was good.) to show us how to work hard and how to take a break.

It is important that you take a day or at least part of a day and do nothing. Each year, you must get away and take a vacation, and spending time away from the kids occasionally is a must. They will be better for it, and so will you. When the boys were little, they would get upset when Brian and I left them and went out of town. They would call us and ask us what we were eating. As they aged, they began to see the importance of rest as our value was being imparted to them, and when we came home, we began to plan a family getaway for the four of us. Now that they are adults, I anticipate that they too will value time away and learn to rest.

Always keep something fun on the calendar to look forward to. It is life giving and hopeful. It does not have to be expensive. I remember taking our coin jar and freebie coupons and driving around town collecting our free and discounted food items. We had a blast! You do not have to have a lot of money to take a break. After all, parenting is a marathon, not a sprint, right? Build time into your schedule to take care of yourself and learn to rest well. I think I am just so much nicer and I seem to love better when I get a little break. I bet you are too.

I realized a few years ago that in my house of men, there were no pink things. No girlie pillows or blankets, bows or lace—so I bought myself a pink towel. It was obviously mine, and I loved it. I have since made it a point to buy things that are just for me, in pink or purple. I am not the only one who likes such beauty. Someone is crazy about pink sunsets, purple flowers, turquoise waters. The Creator is enthralled with beauty. He, himself, is beautiful, and he loves his beautiful creation. He loves beautiful hearts and beautiful things. He loves jewels so much that he made the gates in heaven out of single pearls, and the streets are paved with gold. The Bible speaks of the beauty of the Lord, his robe, his hair, his temple. He is pure and he loves beauty.

Could it be in our society that Christian women have been made to feel that they are supposed to be good and holy but not value outward beauty or beautiful material things? Let me contend that we are made in the very image of God, and we are drawn to beauty because he is. As mothers, especially mothers with boys, we must allow ourselves to value the beautiful and lovely and, yes, girlie things in life without shame. If you need to color your hair, you should do it. Get your nails done or buy a lovely outfit that makes you look great. Do not forget about yourself. God thinks you are beautiful, and you should feel that way.

In my attempts to value rest and beauty, there is one thing I have had to learn—something I am still learning. Learn to say no. You cannot do everything, or you will never rest. Even Jesus did not heal all the sick people, and he was the Son of God. I have a little phrase that I have used over the years, and I have no idea who said it originally, but it has been a guide rail to my crazy busy life: "Do what is important, not what is urgent." The urgent things will always be there. People need you to volunteer. The school needs you. People in the community will fill your schedule if you do not take hold of it yourself. You must decide what is important to you—what you will wish you had invested in ten years from now—and say no to most everything else. If we do all the urgent things, we will fail to do what is truly important.

Is there a chance that you have lost your identity? Do you feel like a mommy machine, a milk machine, or a manager of your household janitorial services? You are not alone. I have sat and cried on my couch more than one time in search of that fun, thin, smiling girl I used to be. She is in there, I tell you. Maybe you could buy yourself a pink towel and wipe that pretty face of yours and know from those who have walked this way before that you are valuable, and you are more than a boy mom. You have hopes and dreams and talents, and you are really, really good at some things. Being a mom is supercool, but being an individual is cool too, and you can do both.

Heads up: this is going to sound superspiritual, but this is the real deal. Find your significance and your security in Jesus and allow him to be all that you need. You will make it through this time in parenting. Maybe you are frightened to let your son drive; maybe he is making bad decisions. Maybe you are a grandparent and you do not have the influence that you wish you had in the lives of your grandchildren. Let God be the place that you run for all of your value and importance and safety, and he will give you grace and sort it all out and let you find yourself again. You are so valuable. Take care of you.

> *He said to them, "Come away by yourselves to a secluded place and rest a while." (Mark 6:31)*

CHAPTER EIGHT

Cutting the Grass with Scissors

(When you don't know that your boy has ADD.)

I HAVE THREE AMAZING MEN IN MY HOUSE—AND ALL THREE OF THEM have attention deficit disorder (ADD). And what about that little *H* that sneaks up and adds *hyperactivity* (ADHD) to the mix? Here are some random and, hopefully, helpful thoughts for those of you who have a son with ADD. And for those of you who think you should skip over this chapter, well, I too never considered that my second grader had a diagnosis! What? He could focus like it was his job; he was smart and he had excellent grades.

In walks his teacher, Mrs. New. "Are you saying that you think Zach has ADD?" I asked. I had been an elementary teacher, and I knew about those little boys who could not sit still, the ones who incessantly clicked their pencils on their desks. Mrs. New informed me that Zach stood in the back of the classroom. He could not stay in his seat. But because she was so incredibly loving to him and allowed him to do whatever he needed to do to be successful in her classroom, let's just say that she earned my respect and appreciation, so I took her advice and had him tested by a psychologist.

We visited Dr. Bird six times. We filled out paper work and Zach took tests, but our final visit was a pulling back of the curtain, a marked moment that threw light on our situation. As Dr. Bird read his summary, he explained that ADD is inherited from a parent or grandparent. Immediately and humorously I suspected Brian's mom! Brian, however, and unbeknownst to me, knew that it was himself. He listened to the description of the way Zach's brain worked and could relate. This began a journey for us, a journey of discovering truth that would eventually bring freedom and understanding for our whole family.

People with ADD are usually very smart and creative. They can be full of energy and adventure. Our house was almost always fun when the boys were growing up, and I don't think I can remember the last time I was bored! I'm learning that people with ADD may give answers that are different, but their answers are not necessarily wrong. They think out of the conventional box. However, I have noticed two ways they tend to measure themselves. They either think they are too complicated (and may be bored out of their minds) *or* think they are stupid (because they have to work so much harder than everyone else). The "bored" student is often labeled "bad." They are voted class clown. They have ten thousand thoughts going through their heads all at once. They can barely sit still.

The second type may think they are stupid, and they may be relieved to be diagnosed with ADD, as it will confirm that they are actually smart. They too have ten thousand thoughts swirling through their brains, and they are used to spending about ten hours writing a paper that takes everyone else one or two hours to write. Because they have to work so hard, they are often accustomed to having to go the extra mile. They are out to prove something to all those who never thought they could excel.

People with ADD may lose their keys two or three times a day. They will most likely turn around and walk away in the middle of your conversation and not even know they did it. They may thrive on taking risks and running late; they often embrace procrastination and change. However, the rush makes them work better and faster. They are typically adrenaline junkies who find danger or excitement very appealing.

Here are some things that you can do to help your son and others you love who have ADD:

Summarize your thoughts. If you continue to go into detail, you will frustrate them.

Don't make fun of them. Don't tell them how dumb they are because they can't find their keys—again. Just buy a nice key hook, and when they don't use it, say, "I'm putting your keys on the key hook, OK?"

Be willing to go to a psychologist and get a correct diagnosis. You may have to try medicine—many different ones. Some medicines work for some people and make others weep. Seriously. It's trial and error. Be patient. At one point, all three men in my house were taking ADD meds. Now none of them are. For various reasons, they have all stopped taking them. But the time they spent finding the correct medication and experimenting with how it affected their focus was incredibly educational and, in the moment, a rescue of sorts.

Taylor was the last to be tested by a psychologist. He is not hyper, loud, or outwardly nonfocused; however, in his head, thoughts are running at megaspeed. Who would know? He was diagnosed with classic ADD in high school and began to take medicine. I will never forget the conversation we had. When Taylor shared with us the difference the medicine was making in his ability to focus on his schoolwork, he compared it to using scissors to cut the grass for his whole life, and suddenly, he felt as though he had been given a lawnmower. Wow. I thought him quite articulate to be able to capture that kind of word picture. I did not understand that simple tasks seemed so arduous and overwhelming. If I had known sooner, don't you think I would have wanted to free him up from the proverbial scissors? If your child needed glasses, you would not hesitate to go to the eye doctor, so I implore you to consider what medicine could do for your son, if and only if his doctor or psychologist recommends it.

I thought Zach was quite disobedient, and I thought I was the worst parent until I found out that he has ADHD. By the time he got up the stairs, he had forgotten what I had asked him to do. I was so conflicted. I didn't know if I should discipline him. I actually cried when I was told he had ADHD because I realized it was not his fault and I was not a bad mother.

Just because your son can concentrate on a video game, technology, or a movie doesn't mean that he can concentrate on important nonstimulating things. Our doctor explained to us that having ADD was like having an empty swimming pool in your head. A thought had to swim from one end to the other to actually be remembered or acted upon. There is no water in ADD pools, so thoughts are not turned into actions that can be carried out. Two things fill the pool: adrenaline and medicine. Interesting.

Teach your son to discern between truth and lies. It may be stimulating to believe a lie. A lie Satan wants him to believe. A lie that says he is too complicated or messy. God is a truth teller, and we want to listen to him.

Encourage. Encourage. Encourage. And Pray. God made you and those you love so perfectly and uniquely. They can do difficult, amazing things. They might just need more help doing it. Some of the smartest businesspeople, doctors, inventors, athletes, and world leaders have ADD.

We need people who do not conform and who refuse to believe those who tell them that what they dream cannot be done. Who cares what other people think? Who cares what other parents do? Who cares if someone thinks you do too much for your kids? You know them. Do what works for your family because God has a great plan for all of you, and you can love and encourage and cheer, as your boy just might change the world.

> *You made all the delicate, inner parts of my body and knit me together in my mother's womb. Thank you for making me so wonderfully complex! Your workmanship is marvelous— how well I know it. (Psalm 139:13–14 NLT)*

CHAPTER NINE

Fight Night

(Bad parenting and the grace of God.)

I WAS IN THE KITCHEN WHEN ZACH RACED UPSTAIRS FROM THE BASE-ment. He was out of breath; the blood on his face had dripped down to his shirt. "Mom, I'm fine! I'm fine!" he yelled, wiping his bloody face with his arm. "Don't make me stop! I promise I'm OK!" Knowing the history of his frequent nosebleeds, I believed him, wiped him down, and sent him back downstairs. Fight night was happening in my basement! Now, I am not going to win any blue parenting rib-bons for admitting this story, but we allowed our thirteen-year-old to take his birthday money and buy two pairs of real boxing gloves, headgear, and mouthpieces. He handwrote a sign with his fight night rules and posted it in our basement.

Zach is a gatherer of people. His ability to network and motivate the seventh graders in the neighborhood was impressive, and he was a man with a plan. We decided that all fight night participants must wear a mouthpiece and that we must have permission from each of their parents. I called each fighter's mother and explained precisely that the boys who participated in fight night fully expected to beat the crap out of each other. "Would you like to give your son permission to beat and be beaten in our basement?" I asked. "Sure, that will be fine," the willful mothers replied. Clearly, I was not the only crazy mom in the neighborhood! The permissions given were given with such a lack of reluctance and in such a carefree and non-thought-through manner that one might think I was asking the boys to gather for sidewalk chalk drawing or a piano sing-along. These mothers did not care. They too were raising energetic boys, and fight night was fine by them.

Some of the boys scurried to drop out before the big event started. Only the grittiest of the neighborhood showed up for our first (and last) fight night, but it was a night to remember! It was real, and it was fierce. Zach broke his friend's nose. Our concrete basement wall splattered with blood told the story of the famous event that would be remembered for years to come. Tall boys, short boys, heavy-weights, and featherweights came together for a man-sized event that night, and each left knowing in his heart that indeed, he was a beast.

However much our parenting skills may have been in question, one thing was very clear: fight night and fighting because of anger are two very different things, and angry fighting was not allowed.

Now, just because angry fighting was not allowed does not mean that it did not happen. I was personally shocked to see boys fight, probably because I grew up in a home with two little sisters and a brother who is almost eleven years younger than me. No one was allowed to fight in my house. Brian, on the other hand, grew up in a house with two boys, and they fought all the time. As Brian likes to say, when our boys were growing up, our house was like the Middle East. You never knew when a war was going to break out. Now I am happy and humbled to say that our grown boys are best friends.

In homes with strong wills, "same ol', same ol'" disciplinary measures quickly become obsolete, so in the spirit of ingenuity, Brian came up with a great corrective action for fighting or disrespect. Brian had a woodpile in the backyard, and he devised a plan to have the boys work together to move the pile from one side of the yard to the other when they could not get along. I remember peering out the window on several occasions, watching our elementary-age off-spring partner together to move that heavy pile yet again to another spot in the backyard. I must admit that we found it humorous and tried not to let the boys see us laugh as we watched them help each other complete their project together. Dropping logs. Chucking logs. Getting their anger out. Engaging in physical activity. Having time to think about their actions. Persevering together in unity. All the components to a great disciplinary idea were at work in the simple moving of a pile of logs. Right? Gosh, what brilliant parents we thought we were!

Well, it was not long after the days of the moving of the pile that Zach's allergies and asthma hit an all-time high. After about a zillion allergy-testing tiny needles, it was determined that he was allergic to basically every grass, weed, and tree. Our brilliant parenting move had been making him worse. He was allergic to the pile! Genius us. Sometimes you just do the best you can, right?

Sometimes parents want to think that their kids are compliant because they themselves are stellar parents. We knew from the beginning that if our strong-willed boys ever turned out to be great men, it would not be because of us; it would be because of the grace of God. When you cannot give yourself credit for the outcome, chances are you may be more likely to humbly recognize God's grace.

We are not going to do this parenting thing perfectly. We are all going to make mistakes. Don't beat yourself up. Don't beat each other up. But do pray for wisdom. I love James chapter 1, where it talks about asking God for wisdom. Like I mentioned earlier, the Bible actually tells us to ask God for wisdom if any of us lack it, and I think most of us parents will be the first to admit that we lack wisdom. The amazing thing about James chapter 1 is that God promises to give us wisdom when we ask for it. He doesn't hold back, and he doesn't make fun of us for asking. Isn't that comforting? God has given you everything you need to parent the boy he gave you. Whether you are a single parent, a stepparent, a new parent, or a grandparent, you can relax and ask God for his abundant wisdom and grace. He will give it because that is the kind of God he is.

> *If you need wisdom, ask our generous God,*
> *and he will give it to you. (James 1:5)*

I have had the privilege of raising three wonderful boys, two of whom are now married to two amazing women. Often, I would hear girls talk about their evil mothers-in-law, and I knew I never wanted to be labeled as that. It was so important to me to work at trying to be the best I could be. Even though I was far from perfect, I've listed just a few things that I tried to apply during the years. *Cut the apron strings.* Realize that your input is no longer the primary influence in your son's life. *Compliment your daughter-in-law.* Never criticize. Let her know what a positive influence she has been in your son's life. *Only give advice when asked.* Your unsolicited advice could come across as a threat to her. *Accept her for who she is.* Don't try to change her. Encourage and love her unconditionally. *Pray for your daughter-in-law* rather than questioning or criticizing her. Bring the issues to God and love her like you would your own daughter. Remember, when you are raising a son, you are raising someone's husband and father, so raise him well.

—Judy Bloye Hitchcock

CHAPTER TEN

Everything Is a Sword

(Saying yes to as much as possible.)

THE PIRATES OF THE CARIBBEAN IS ONE OF MY FAVORITE RIDES AT Disney World. Do you remember the pirate in jail who is beckoning the dog with the keys? I marvel at the lifelike figure whose hairy leg dangles over the bridge as he chugs his rum. He joins his friends in a jolly chorus. "A pirate's life for me . . ." he sings as our tiny boat sails under the darkened cave-like overpass. It smells musty, and the water becomes a mist that summons us to join the life of the marauders. As we exit, we are redirected through the gift shop, a clever idea. If the pirates don't get your booty, the gift shop will! We pass by hats, hooks, and parrots until my elementary-age boys spy the only toy that continually grabs their interest: the swords. We are eager to purchase two of them, and we exit the gift shop unscathed.

For the rest of the day, our boys fought playfully with their toy blades. Jumping on park benches, pouncing in the lines, grimacing and poking, these little pirates snarfed down their lunches to resume their scrappy duel.

After our family left the most magical of kingdoms and returned home from vacation, even the more common and ancillary items had the ability to morph into a sword. If we were outside, the boys found sticks and instantly began to wave them as swords. If we went to a restaurant, the straws became swords. Even fish sticks had the capability to jump off the plate at lunchtime and artfully transform into steel blades.

One of my favorite sword stories is set in the spirit of Christmas. With the sights and smells of the holidays, even youngsters can develop a true sense of gratitude and the sincere desire to give to others. From the time they were little, the boys wanted to buy each other Christmas gifts. They spent their own money, saved from their allowance, and blissfully shopped at the Dollar Tree for the perfect gift. I took both boys to the same dollar store, one at a time, and observed as they scrutinized the toy aisle, each separately contemplating what the store had to offer and which singular toy would not only bring the most joy but also be the biggest hit on Christmas morning. After carefully examining the balls, bubbles, and action figures, each chose the same exact gift for the other—the sword. Brian and I kept their secret until they each opened their presents from each other, and they both were elated—a sword! They hugged each other tightly and drew their gifts in the ultimate joyful Christmas clash!

When our boys each turned thirteen, we threw them a big party, and Brian presented them with a real Celtic sword. Before they arrived at their party, they took a walk that Brian had planned out. He had the men who had most influenced their lives walk with them one-fourth of a mile each. As they walked, they each had a conversation with the boys about a specific characteristic of a great man. We wanted them to speak truth over our sons on the first day that they became teenagers—a rite of passage into manhood. Their swords are still a representation of what took place on that special day of celebration. In fact, their swords represent strength and ability, skill and victory. It is vitally important for boys to know the power of the sword yet understand that trusting in their own abilities and skills will not ultimately deliver. The psalmist acknowledges that his sufficiency comes from God alone, who strengthens and delivers.

"I do not count on my sword to save me," he says (Ps. 44:6–7 NLT). Though these swords of Celtic genealogy represent strength and confidence, we must remind our sons that no amount of proficiency or skill can be trusted to be the source of identity or worth. The security and significance of the strongest men must be firmly rooted in a powerful God.

The playfulness of little boys has always intrigued me, and the noises they have the ability to make, the motor-like sounds, are perfectly innate. What is it about those active little boys that brings out the husher in us mamas? "No! Stop. Be quiet," we say. "Get down. Stop climbing. Don't jump on the bed. Sit still. No, because I said so, that's why!"

Do you remember pull-string dolls? When you pull the attached string, the doll repeats a series of prerecorded, automated responses. Similarly, I can picture the natural activity of little boys pulling the strings of our nerves, which must be attached to our mouths, from which automated responses often emerge.

Recently, our family watched some of our old home movies. They are beautiful and telling. As I watched myself, I must say I was dismayed by how much I talked. I constantly gave commands to my boys. I cannot imagine how much I must have exhausted not only them but also the other people who were listening to me. I wanted to reach back in time through the home movie screen and gently say, "Be quiet! Let them play."

It is not just the little boys who bring out our nos. The big boys remind us that we are not so much in control. Why do we want to say so many nos to them? It may be because they are not realistic. They do not have enough life experience. They often want to go places with people we do not know. We hear stories of bad influences, and we may want to whisk our good children away from all the things that are unfamiliar to us. "Please, stay calm and innocent and near home with your old, boring parents," we may wish. Perhaps we would like to insure with our nos that everything is going to be OK.

As the generation gap expands, I am reminded that I do not clearly understand the nos that this younger generation is having to say on their own every day. In many ways, they have it easier than we did, but there are so many things that they are dealing with that were just not on my radar as a young person. The world has changed, and good kids are saying no to a lot of bad things. The good news is that I am watching young people become leaders and choose good. These millennials get a bad rap sometimes, but I believe that God always raises up people in every generation to lead boldly. There are so many things to which we and our sons have to say no. What if we could be moms who say yes to as much as possible? What if we could lead with a yes? Certainly say no to sinful things and harmful things, but let's decide together that we will work on considering the *Y* word before we blurt out a no.

Yes, you may walk in the mud puddle, why not? Yes, you may wear socks that do not match, why not? Yes, you may eat dessert first and stay up half an hour later, and yes, we will listen to your side of the story. You may jump on the hotel bed as high as you want to, and yes, you may skip some vegetables that make you throw up.

When we say no, we want it to be for a good reason, and they need to know that we mean it. I want to encourage you that we can be fun moms, stepmoms, and grandmoms that lead with a yes as much as possible.

> *For all of God's promises have been fulfilled in Christ with a resounding, "Yes!" (2 Corinthians 1:20 NLT)*

I became a stepmom to the cutest little three-year-old boy anyone has ever seen. Yes, I know I'm probably a little biased, but he had blonde hair and these giant brown eyes that could just melt your heart. Since I was an "instant" mom, there was no time to gradually work into knowing how to raise a child, which led to a lot of mistakes for which I am incredibly thankful for grace and forgiveness. The best piece of advice that I received was from my dad, who overheard me repeatedly telling my stepson, Bradley, no one day when we were all at the pool, for things like jumping on the stairs, splashing water, and flipping himself over the handrail. He told me that little boys are active and adventurous and that I needed to let him be a boy and that the worst thing that could happen is that he could hurt himself, but so what—that was how he would learn. He said that if I kept telling him no for fear of him getting hurt, he would grow up to be cautious and afraid to try anything. Well, I am happy to report that he did grow up (without too many trips to the ER) to be an amazing young man who is fun-loving and full of adventure and greatness.

—Ruth Wittenbrook, stepmom

CHAPTER ELEVEN

No Sceered Men

(Overcoming fear.)

DID YOU KNOW THAT BABIES ARE BORN WITH ONLY TWO INNATE FEARS? From birth, we have the fear of falling and the fear of loud noises. If you hold a newborn baby away from you, the child will wave their arms in reaction to the fear of being dropped. We all know that loud noises are terrifying to babies; we tiptoe around newborns. Their fears are certainly valid. Other fears, they say, are mostly learned. Aditi Subramaniam is a mother and a neuroscience PhD. In *Psychology Today*, she describes the "amygdala, an almond shaped structure in our brain that plays an important role in coordinating fear response. It is the part of the brain that intervenes between the regions concerned with the bodily expression of emotion and the areas of the brain that are concerned with conscious feeling."[1] It monitors the difference between our body reacting to a possibly dangerous situation and our having the time to decide if it is something that we should actually fear. Whatever that little almond-shaped part of our brain signals, we can accept the fact that fear is real and our bodies were made to assess it.

Certainly, some fears are healthy. It is our responsibility to teach our boys that running into the busy road is dangerous, as they could easily be hit by a car. We must have a genuine fear of touching the stove when it is hot or our lack of fear will result in a burned hand. It is my observation, however, that mothers sometimes have the tendency to create fear in their boys, and in turn, our sons grow up to have fears that hinder them from being all that they are created to be. Should we follow our boys around with baby wipes and hand sanitizer? Should we keep them from jumping off anything higher than six inches off the ground? We may think that we are keeping them safe and making ourselves feel better, but I would argue that, in the long run, if we tell them how scary everything is, we will hold them back in life. We do not want our boys to become inhibited, constrained, and fearful men.

Men are wired to be protectors. They fight in wars and they rescue. They stand up for what is right, and they have the confidence to talk to women. They work hard and believe in themselves. They are not scared of raindrops or puppies or blood or threatening circumstances. They are made in the very image of the God who is not fearful of anything at all. God is not self-conscious, reticent, or apprehensive. He is decisive, strong, and capable. God's perfect love, in fact, "casts out all fear" (1 John 4:18). Our sons are made in his likeness.

I recently did a very informal survey on social media and asked, "What do you think is a primary cause of fear in boys and men?" Here are some of the responses I received:

- Boys have watched fear being modeled, and in turn, they become fearful.
- The fear of failure is one of the greatest fears that men seem to have.
- They compare themselves to successful leaders in their homes and workplaces.
- Success is about comparison, and a man's self-worth is connected to his accomplishments.

- Expectations are often so high that no one can achieve them, and that creates fear.
- Men fear rejection.
- The fear of what other people think is a genuine fear that many boys grow up with.
- Men may fear not being good enough.
- The enemy creates fear.
- Men have a huge responsibility as leaders of the home.
- The fear of being fearful and appearing weak is a fear in itself.
- Not being able to provide for their families creates stress and fear.

I then asked, "How can parents help instill fearlessness in their boys?" People responded with these ideas:

- Parents drive away fear by speaking words of confidence and courage.
- Teaching perseverance through little failures and teaching them to take risks dispels fear.
- Push through fear and do it anyway.
- Lead by example.
- Instill self-worth.
- Allow boys to work out their feelings.
- Inspire them.
- Make goals and focus on reaching them so they will learn success.
- Teach them who they are in Christ and the authority they have over fear (2 Tim. 1:7).
- Teach them to control their thoughts (2 Cor. 10:3–5).
- Let them be boys and play hard and make decisions and lead.

- A father's words of affirmation resound for decades.
- Speak the Bible over your sons when they go to bed (Josh. 1:9).
- Men in their lives need to give good direction.

There are many elements of truth in the above lists. As I read them, I could almost sense the history that came from many of them. Men explained the pain of rejection, comparison, and failure, and ladies answered, some of them desiring freedom for the men they love who have been held back by apprehension. I would concede that all have been affected by fear.

There are five things that stand out to me as a mother as I partner with you in pushing through fear ourselves and helping our boys to be fearless men.

Cultivate a Sense of Gratitude

There is something about thankfulness that dispels fear. Perhaps it lies in the history of good things that happened and the recollection of things that were once feared and turned out to be OK. Perhaps it turns our hearts to the One to whom we give thanks, the One who is ultimately fearless and calls us to faith over fear. Nonetheless, our gratefulness is a prequel to peace of mind. Philippians 4:6–7 says, "Do not be anxious about anything, but in every situation, by prayer and petition, with *thanksgiving*, present your requests to God. And the peace of God, which transcends all understanding, will guard your hearts and your minds in Christ Jesus" (my emphasis). I know that fear can make us feel like we are losing our minds. It is good to know that gratitude is an important ingredient in the recipe that results in our minds being kept and guarded by the peace that only God can give.

Understand That Fear Is a Liar

Fear will cause our boys to believe lies and to lie to themselves. I like the lyrics of the song "Fear Is a Liar" by Zach Williams. He personifies fear by giving fear human attributes. Fear tells us that we are not good enough, that we are not enough, that we are not worthy, strong, or loved. Fear speaks to us and to our sons with words of shame, and isolation: "He will take your breath, stop you in your steps . . . rob your rest, steal your happiness." Williams encourages us to "cast [our] fear into the fire, 'cause fear, he is a liar."[2]

As parents, we have to address fear. We have to talk about it and speak the truth and quote the Bible. Our boys must know that fear will lie to them, and they must choose in their most hesitant moments to grab on to the coattails of our faith and make it their own. They will be used to hearing us speak the truth, and it will resonate in their most fearful moments.

Cultivate Twenty Seconds of Insane Courage

Our family watched the movie *We Bought a Zoo*. Since then, we have adopted a phrase from the movie to muster brief spurts of courage. When we have to send a bold email, or communicate through a challenging text message, or make the call, or just say no, someone in the family will say, "Twenty seconds of insane courage!" Sometimes twenty seconds of uncharacteristic boldness will be all it takes to make the move. Pray and be bold for twenty seconds. Your son can ask out the most beautiful girl if he only has twenty seconds of boldness. If he can push through his fear for only twenty seconds, he can do and say things he never thought he could. Encourage him to apply for the job, raise his hand with the answer, get the membership, or make the purchase. Prayer plus twenty seconds of insane courage just might change everything!

Learn to Fear God

Fearing God does not mean that we are afraid of him; rather, according to the *Olive Tree Blog*, it means

> to be in reverent awe of His holiness, to give Him complete reverence and to honor him as the God of great glory, majesty, purity and power... God instructs his followers to teach their children to fear him by training them to hate sin and to love God's commands (Dt 4:10; 6:1–2, 6–9). The Bible often states that "the fear of the Lord is the beginning of wisdom" (Ps 111:10). A Christian's basic goal for his or her children should be that they learn to live by God's principles of wisdom (Pr 1:1–6). Teaching them to fear the Lord is a critical first step.[3]

As we teach our boys to fear God by standing in awe of him, he will become bigger in their eyes, and earthly fears will seem smaller.

Do It Scared

I am pretty sure that most people who do great things are afraid. The difference is, they do it anyway. We cannot wait until we feel cozy and confident to do the bold thing. Talk to your boys about doing it scared. Show them examples of men who were scared but fought anyway and won. Do you think our great military leaders have ever been terrified? Of course they have been, but they fight anyway. Do you think that actors, singers, writers, speakers, and creators are scared to put forth their works in front of a crowd of spectators? Of course they are self-conscious and apprehensive, but they do it anyway. Do athletes, doctors, first responders, teachers, mechanics, and entrepreneurs deal with fear? Absolutely. Leaders and winners are all fearful, but they push through their fears and do the hard thing. That is what makes them great.

Scientists affirm that loud noises and the fear of falling are innate, but do you know that there is another debatable fear that many seem to think is inborn? The fear in question is the fear of being alone. Maybe the fear of loneliness has not made it into the science books as definitively innate, but we can all agree that it sneaks right in there at a very early age and scares the boldness and confidence out of each and every one of us. From infancy, humans do not usually do well alone. Maybe we could do the bold thing if we were not alone. Maybe our boys could chase their dreams if the chase was not out on the ugly limb of loneliness. Maybe we could hear a voice of confidence, dispelling fear, if we were not alone. Friend, the best news of the day is that you are not alone. You are not alone in parenting, and you are not alone in the deep, deep dreams of your heart that you fear will never become reality. You are not alone in breaking the cycle of poverty or racism or abuse or fatherlessness or sickness. You are not alone, and your son will never ever be alone, even when you are not around. For the God of the universe dispels all fears when he whispers, "Do not be afraid" (Deut. 31:8 NLT).

> *I will never leave you. I will never abandon you. (Hebrews 13:5 NLT)*

In my line of work, people often wonder if I am scared to go to the places I go and do the work that I do. Really? I am the mom of two boys. What could possibly scare me? But seriously, raising boys is not what should scare us. Failing to raise future men, husbands, fathers, and leaders of faith and integrity is what should scare us. And that's what should challenge us to embrace the high calling of being a #boymom.

—Noel Yeatts, president, World Help

CHAPTER TWELVE

Pierced and Tatted

(The four things we want our boys to know.)

WE DO NOT WANT TO THINK THAT OUR SWEET BABIES WILL SUFFER one day. No one wants to imagine that in our absence, our boys may deal with persecution, insurmountable grief, sickness, loss, financial challenges, stress, or divorce. In their infancy, we guarded them against every wrong, every possible thing that could hurt them, but as they grow, we innately know that our ability to protect them is not enough. The question is, then, What is going to sustain them in their most difficult moments?

Will your son be able to stand firm in the face of heartache and danger because he kept a list of rules? Will he be sustained in his most difficult moments because he cleaned his room, ate organic, went to church, and didn't get a tattoo? Your structure and his ability to not embarrass the family—will that be what you will count on to be the rock and strength he needs when you are not around to fix his inevitable pain? Will "being good" get him through the challenges of life?

The answer is no. These things will not be heavy enough to reach the very soul of your boy and fill a void; heal open wounds; or rescue him from suicide, depression, or overwhelming loss. There is something about motherhood that makes us want to control. I want to provide a simple to-do list that I can put my trust in as the guardrail to a painless life for my sons. A false and breakable hope that sounds like it might have the ability to be a godlike charm to keep away fear and evil. We wrongfully assure ourselves that if we do all the things and they do all that we say, they will emerge with a strength that will surely be enough.

Here is the truth: only the grace and love of Jesus will be enough during your son's most difficult moments, so spend your energy and your very little bit of time pointing him to the One who will be there in your absence and will have the ability to rescue him and be every single powerful thing he needs.

Pivot your thinking away from "We don't want to be messy" and "Please do not embarrass me." When you look back, you will not care if he chewed his Flintstone vitamin quickly enough. You will not care if his sock drawer was organized by color or if his penmanship reached your lofty standard. You will want to know, however, that he learned to find his identity in what God says about him instead of what the kids at school said. You will find rest in the fact that your boy saturated his life in Jesus and learned to walk in faith even though he could not see what lay ahead.

Even as our boys morph into men, we have the ability to turn their eyes to truth and to encourage them to anchor themselves deeply in the truth of God's Word.

There are four powerful things that we want our sons, Taylor and Zach, to know, and we are working to weave these things into our conversations through the years. We have not put them on a chart or a spreadsheet. They do not hold a place on our refrigerator. Instead, we have deliberately chosen to be aware of naturally occurring moments to plant these truths into the foundational soil of their lives and ours. Here are the four things we want them to know.

God Loves You Unconditionally

Ephesians 3:19 is one of my favorite verses. In fact, I had the reference tattooed on my foot! "May you experience the love of Christ, though it is too great to understand fully. Then you will be made complete with all the fullness of life and power that comes from God." Fullness of life. Power. That is what we all want, and that is what we want for our sons, right? Would we want a life that is less full? Do we want our boys to live a life void of fullness? Of course not. Then we must point them to what? We must point them to the fact that they are loved inexpressibly by the God who created the universe. He will take it from there. He can help them experience that love in a way that we cannot, but it is our job to lead them to that love as an answer to their questions, and as a result, they will be made complete with power and a full life. This is much more than our good parenting can guarantee. This is God stuff, and it rescues and makes whole things that are broken.

You Can Trust Him Completely

Proverbs 3:5–6 tells us, "Trust in the Lord with all your heart and lean not on your own understanding. In all your ways acknowledge him and he will direct your paths." Whether you are interacting with your son in a conversation about preschool friends, middle school sports, being left out, high school prom, or his career, the fact that God is trustworthy is a foundational truth that we must repeat and remind them of for the rest of our lives. They come to us, and that is what they get. Point them to the fact that in the scenario of their age-appropriately stress-filled life, God can be trusted. And as we do this, we are actually depositing truth in their hearts—truth that will come out when we are not around.

He Will Never Leave You

According to Hebrews 13:5b, "I will never fail you. I will never abandon you." The fear of abandonment is multiplying in our world. Kids are watching their friends feel abandoned through divorce. Even classmates on the playground "abandon" and change friend groups. Breakups, gossip, and lies. No one wants to feel abandoned at any age. Abandonment is a primary fear that we all deal with. Your son, whether he is two or forty-two, deals with these issues in our society, and as parents, we will partner with God by modeling and instilling the truth that God is always, always, always with us.

Everything You Need Is in Christ

Colossians 2:9–10 says, "For in Christ lives all the fullness of God in a human body. So you also are complete through your union with Christ, who is the head over every ruler and authority." You are *complete*. That means that everything you need is in Jesus. Everything your boy needs, he gets through Jesus. What a foundational truth! May we be so satisfied in Jesus alone in our own lives that our faith is contagious, and our boys will know in their souls that Jesus truly is enough.

As you talk in the kitchen, as you bandage a skinned knee, as you listen after a first date, as you wipe a tear or celebrate a victory, keep these truths in the forefront. It is not the little day-to-day rules that will ever be our anchor. We and our sons will only be anchored in the truth of God's Word, and it is in him that our hope lies.

If our sons got one hundred piercings and had purple mohawks *and* grasped the accurate views of God and these four truths to anchor their lives, well, that would be fine by me.

> *God will do this for he is faithful to do what he says. (1 Corinthians 1:9 NLT)*

God has truly blessed me with daughters and a son to raise for him. Our daughters have all grown into strong leaders of people. Yet you raise daughters realizing they will need to be supportive, encouragers, and followers of their leader-husbands. Raising a son, your purpose is to raise a leader. That son will grow to be the leader in his home, confident and willing to step out there with decisions and opportunities. (Either way, train your child to learn God's Word and they'll have a head start.)

—Nancy Mills (my mom)

CHAPTER THIRTEEN

Dancing with a Dolphin

(Sometimes experiences are better than gifts.)

THE SAND SQUISHED BETWEEN OUR TOES, AND THE HEAT FROM THE December Nassau sun fell gently upon us. We were next in line to the dolphin encounter, the surprise gift we gave our boys for Christmas. We had all decided that instead of getting gifts, we would get away, and so we found an affordable three-day cruise and added a little dolphin experience. Who knew that dolphins were so intelligent? As we stood as a family in our space in the water, the trainer ordered the dolphin to shake hands and to dance and to kiss us on the cheek. He swam like a rocket underwater and leaped through the air doing flips and standing upright on his tail fin. We fed him fish and posed for pictures with all the smiles! We had a blast on our trip and made so many memories. Even the bad weather that caused us to miss out on our second fun day propelled us to the dining room, where we ate the best meal of our lives.

So many of our finest memories together have been about doing something fun and out of the ordinary. I have loved investing time and resources into experiences. Sometimes the bonds they create stay with us longer than a thing we could buy and wrap.

We decided when the boys were little that we would try to visit as many professional baseball stadiums as we could. We have traveled to see the Dodgers, the Braves, the White Sox, the Orioles, the Angels, the Padres, and several more. One time some friends gifted us with a gift card for free flights anywhere in the United States! This was an amazing gift, so we wanted to see just how far we could go. We picked the farthest city that had a baseball team that would be playing a home game the week of our vacation and decided that would be our destination. The Mariners were playing at home in Seattle, and so Seattle it was! I don't remember the score of the game, but I do remember the fun and adventure we had on that trip.

Not every adventure has to cost a lot of money. Sometimes the simplest times together make the best memories and the biggest impact. My growing-up memories consist of making homemade ice cream and eating watermelon in my grandparents' yard while catching lightning bugs. Home movies and board games are inexpensive experiences that bond families together. I remember my dad sculpting sea creatures on the beach while passersby stopped to admire his incredible artwork. Dad had all of us helping with digging and carving using shovels and butter knives. Of course, he gave us all the credit for his talented sand creations. These are the things that matter—the free and fun life that gets lived between all the planned expensive things.

Our family has had the privilege of using my sister-in-law's family cabin for over twenty years. When I walk into the cabin, I can see with my memory's eye my little boys jumping in the baby swing in the doorway by the kitchen. I remember my sister-in-law being pregnant with my niece, my boys running outside to meet their grandpa unloading Michigan corn from his long motorcycle ride across several states. I see the grandchildren playing on the hammock, and I know that memories were made in that sweet place. The best connections are about being and not so much about doing.

The older I get, the more aware I am of the glue that sticks the experiences to the family and pulls everyone together. That glue is peace. If we can avoid forcing experiences and relax with our boys, they will develop memories of happiness. They will not care if everything was planned and executed with perfection. In her book *The Power of a Positive Mom*, Karol Ladd reminds us, "Sometimes we can become so focused on our efforts to create memories for the future that we fail to enjoy the present! We can ruin a potential family memory by our overzealous efforts to make sure everything is 'just right.'"[1] I know that I can struggle with this, and as a mom of adult sons, I am trying to chill out and savor the naturally occurring fun times we have together.

Many years ago, I read a book entitled *Raising Faithful Kids in a Fast-Paced World* by Dr. Paul Faulkner. Dr. Faulkner and his wife, Gladys, interviewed thirty highly successful families and documented exactly what appeared to make them so successful in raising their kids. Could people have brilliant careers and top-notch families at the same time? The Faulkners found that almost all thirty families said and did the same things. Although basically instinctive, their actions were very intentional. In their book, the Faulkners say that "traditions have five basic benefits: they give us a way to define ourselves; they provide stability; they enhance flexibility; they help us maintain high values; and they create a field of dialogue."[2] I love the dialogue part. It means that we have stuff to talk about. We can laugh and "remember when" because we decided to make a tradition. We have history in common, even when we are far away from each other. But to think that traditions would enhance flexibility sounds contradictory. Traditions could appear to make a family set in their ways and therefore less flexible, but check out Faulkner's thoughts:

> This may sound strange, but there's really no contradiction between flexibility and stability. Tradition is like the vaulting

box that anchors the vaulting pole. A man runs down a runway and plants his pole in the box, and it holds his pole; it will not let it shift to the left or the right. And because of the stability of one end of the pole, the vaulter can confidently launch himself with a very flexible pole, fifteen to twenty feet up into the air and over a cross bar. And so it is with our families. A sturdy vaulting box, rich in family tradition and stability, is like a launching pad, enabling your children to venture out into the world in any variety of directions. They may not do the same kind of work we do or live the exact kind of lifestyle we live, but because of their sturdy underpinnings, they can still keep their balance.[3]

What experiences or traditions do you remember from your childhood? Although receiving gifts is one of my top love languages, I value the gifts of time and shared experience more and more. I think Elaine Hardt summed it up well:

Make a memory with your children,
Spend some time to show you care;
Toys and trinkets can't replace those
Precious moments that you share.[4]

> *May you experience the love of*
> *Christ. (Ephesians 3:19 NLT)*

CHAPTER FOURTEEN

Green Van

(Share your needs.
Increase their faith.)

WHEN WE BROUGHT ZACH HOME FROM THE HOSPITAL, I COULD BARELY fit my postpartum hips between the two car seats in the snug backseat of our 1994 Nissan Altima. Not many months after, we resigned to look for a minivan. Quite honestly, we did not want to succumb to being minivan owners, but we could not afford an SUV, and therefore, we mustered up excitement over the search for our new family transportation. As we were accustomed to disclosing our needs and making them family matters, we shared with almost-four-year-old Taylor that we needed a van, and together, the three of us began to pray for it. Taylor decided that our van needed to be green, and so he beseeched the throne of God with his vision of the green van, and who were we to thwart his boldness or his color choice, right?

Not long after the prayers, Brian found the best deals, and we journeyed to check them out. We discovered two options in front of us. One was a good option, and the other was the best option. Can you guess the color of the van that was clearly the best option? Of course, it was green! That day we wrote down the answer to Taylor's prayer in a little notebook that I had entitled "Cool Things God Did." We talked about that green van for over a decade, and it became somewhat of a monument of faith to our preschooler and, in fact, to us as well.

Do you remember the old story of the Israelites crossing the Jordan River? I like this passage in Joshua 4:19–24:

On the tenth day of the first month the people went up from the Jordan and camped at Gilgal on the eastern border of Jericho. And Joshua set up at Gilgal the twelve stones they had taken out of the Jordan. He said to the Israelites, "In the future when your descendants ask their parents, 'What do these stones mean?' tell them, 'Israel crossed the Jordan on dry ground.' For the Lord your God dried up the Jordan before you until you had crossed over. The Lord your God did to the Jordan what he had done to the Red Sea when he dried it up before us until we had crossed over. He did this so that all the peoples of the earth might know that the hand of the Lord is powerful and so that you might always fear the Lord your God."

God instructed Joshua to set up stones in a big pile so that the people would see it and remember and so the kids would ask about it. It would become a teachable moment, a moment to proclaim what a great thing God did for his people. Similarly, we as parents set up stones of remembrance each time we remind our children of how God answered their prayers. We point out times when we see God do something that only he could do. When you acknowledge that "coincidence" was actually a credit to the work of God, you instill faith in your children, and as you write it down in a book or talk about it in the car, you are making deposits of faith in the mind and heart of your boy. Our green van became a stone of remembrance for our family, and our boys still talk about it.

It is interesting that Joshua set up stones in the middle of the Jordan River as well. Check out this thought-provoking verse: "Joshua also set up another pile of twelve stones in the middle of the Jordan at the place where the priests who carried the Ark of the Covenant were standing. And they are there to this day" (Josh. 4:9).

In the middle. He set up stones of remembrance in the middle of the river before he even got to the other side! This means that in the midst of the crisis—in the middle of the challenge, the inconvenience, the trial, the uncertainty—he decided to believe and celebrate as though it was a victory. He undoubtedly had seen God do a thing before, a thing that increased his faith, and he chose to not only call it a win but celebrate in the middle of it! May we be parents who "in the middle of it" can celebrate and point to a history of God's faithful answers to prayers we have prayed (and some we didn't even know to pray), and God will, as only he can, pour a little more faith and hope into the lives of our boys.

Are you in the middle of a difficult time? A season of waiting? Is your son discouraged or anxious or even doubting the goodness of God? Look back and remember a time that God worked something out and talk about it. God likes to take messes and turn them into cool stories. They are usually stories where he is the hero, especially as he most always comes through at the last minute, right?

We can use "stones of remembrance" to tell the stories to future generations, but as we seek to develop men who are firsthand believers, we have to nurture stories that belong to them personally. They have to experience God on their own in order to begin to set up those stones for themselves. Their own experience will have more of an impact than just hearing about what God did for someone else. So how can we as parents help our sons to develop faith on their own?

Serve alongside your boy. Help someone out and let him watch God in action. Save your money together and help a cause. Send him to church camp. Pray with him for his friends. Pray together for opportunities to share your faith and for him to share his faith, and watch God move in conversations at work, in the neighborhood, and at school as he turns those conversations into opportunities. Write down struggles and prayers and answers and victories so that your family sees that God has a track record, a history of being present and at work in the everyday things that matter.

In the late seventies or early eighties, I remember my parents bringing us all into the living room. They told us we were out of money and that we needed to pray that God would come through for us. We prayed sincerely with faith, and we knew that if Mom and Dad said God would help us, then he would.

When I was very little, I spilled the gallon of milk from the top shelf of the refrigerator and Mom cried. It was the only real milk we could afford for a long time, and because I spilled it, we had to drink powdered milk. We had discount lunches and government cheese in high school, and Mom shopped yard sales for 98 percent of our clothing. My parents drove the family car from the time I was in third grade until I was a junior in college. Through these years, I loved life. I developed meaningful relationship skills and a faith in God that would shape my future and strengthen me at the core of my being.

How did this happen? My parents were determined to raise up leaders who would know God. We had to experience for ourselves that God would take care of us and keep his promises. We learned that prayer moves the heart of God—our prayers, not just the prayers of our parents and grandparents.

I remember that one-hundred-dollar bill wrapped around my dad's car door handle when I was five. How do I remember? I remember because my parents included me in our prayers of need, and then they did not fail to include me in the miraculous answers to those prayers. I was there when our missionary support money did not come in, but we talked to God about it and someone brought us cans of food without labels. (I also remember eating those mystery meals that you enjoy when your can has no label on it!) I remember going to McDonald's with our last ten dollars. I remember my sister saying that she was not sure God cared about us, and the next day, all four of us kids were given a five-hundred-dollar savings bond. Twice a year the $17.50 interest checks reminded us that God would provide for our needs.

Seeing the faithfulness of God firsthand in those formative years and knowing for certain that he would not fail us proved to be instrumental in our faith as adults. When I moved to Georgia with my husband to start West Ridge Church, I had no doubt that God would provide for each of our needs in his perfect timing. I had the faith as a young adult to do something risky because it had been instilled in me to do so. This journey of God's provision has been life altering and faith building simply because my parents chose to include us in the story, tell us the challenges, and encourage us to look to God for the answers.

You can totally do this, Mom! Whatever your little messes look like, bring Jesus and the kids into it and put God on the line where he has to come through for them. And he will, you know. And it won't look like you planned for it to look. But he will, through many sweet days and difficult days, cultivate the sweet soil of your son's heart and yours in the meantime. And he will do his best work—maybe with whole milk or a green van—and your story and his will become stones of remembrance.

> *Turn to me and be gracious to me, as is your practice toward those who love your name. (Psalm 119:132 CSB)*

I promise all your words, from "What in the world were you thinking?" to "I love you and believe in you," are shaping the heart of the man your boy will eventually become. It all counts—the little unseen moments of tucking them in, checking their homework, and checking their phones. The moments you absolutely blow it and willingly offer words of "I'm sorry." Raising boys is learning to live life imperfectly, and trusting God's perfect love will always make your love enough in every season.

—Trisha Lopez Davis

CHAPTER FIFTEEN

Don't Act Shocked

(How to get your teenage boys to talk to you.)

REESE DARED ZACH TO PEE ON THE PLAYGROUND IN FIRST GRADE, AND he did. I know because the teacher called me and said that Zach was in trouble and that peeing on the playground was not permitted. Why did he do this? "Because Reese dared me, so I had to do it, Mom. I can't turn down a dare like that." The duo struck again at Johnny's Pizza, their dirty baseball uniforms boasting of a big win. Brilliantly, Johnny's gave a big wad of raw pizza dough to kids at their tables while their food was being prepared. This idea, to me, was genius. Keep those kiddos busy kneading dough while the parents chat and reminisce about the game. Somehow, however, the pizza dough made its way down from the table and to the back of the restaurant, where it was stuffed in the toilet while we, the parents, were obliviously talking. And, yes, the manager and the plumbing can testify that the round, ruinous dough ball was indeed the object of yet another dare. Seriously?! The plumbing was clogged and the boys were in big trouble. I was shocked. Reese and Zach were a humorous duo in elementary school. Reese dared and Zach acted. Crazy boys!

The automated shock factor only increases. We quickly moved to middle school, where a group of girls was rumored to have stuck their newly acquired camera phones down their shirts and took pictures to send to various boys in the sixth grade. What? Again, shock. Where are the mothers of these little loose ladies? Someone should be slapped!

Shock factor increase alert! The stories the boys told me in high school were real jaw droppers. When you hear about students getting stone drunk and friends smoking pot, shock, shock, shock.

Fast-forward to Christian college. I recall the after-the-fact phone calls: "Mom, we didn't tell you because we knew you would be worried or probably say no." Yep. You know me by now, you young adult on your own (and very much not on your own). Shock me more, please! The stories of swimming at midnight in a black hole literally in the pit of a mountain in the dark and almost drowning and the stories of climbing said mountain and the best friend who held on to the rocky side of the mountain by his fingertips, clenching and almost losing his precious life. These are the stories that make our blood pressure rise with worry and shock.

- We drove all night.
- I got paid to eat a bug.
- We threw stink bombs in the girl's dorm.
- I spent an obscene amount of money on a membership to an MMA gym.
- I almost got fired.

Rule #1: Do Not Act Shocked

Mothers, when you hear the stories, if you want your teenage boys to talk to you, do not act shocked. If your jaw drops and you gasp every time your son tells you something bad that he did or something his friend did or something horrible that happened at school, it is very likely that he may not tell you anything else for quite a while. Be shocked on the inside but unemotional on the outside. "Really?

Tell me about that" is your response. No hyperventilating or open-mouthed, wide-eyed stares. You want them to tell you more. You must be cool.

Now, being the recipient of teenage boy conversation is like receiving a medal. If you get any real info, you feel like you have won a little prize. So if you want your teenage boy to talk to you, you must adhere to rule number two.

Rule #2: Do Not Try to Fix Everything

If you shoot off emails and run to the principal's office every time they share with you an injustice or an imperfect remark made by a teacher, they will be embarrassed. If you are "mother to the rescue" for every unfair, scary, disorganized, unhealthy, misrepresented thing in their life, they will stop telling you stuff. "My gosh! Mom is overreacting. Don't tell her another thing," they will think. (Some things you must report, like if someone is being abused or is going to overdose or commit suicide.) You do not need, however, to hightail it to the school if your son got a B when he should have received an A. Let him learn to speak for himself. Your son might talk to you about the things that you are completely unaware of if you do not try to fix all his problems.

Rule #3: Be a Great Listener and Ask Questions

Because we have lived many days, we feel like we can rush in with advice. If we could just sit them down, tell them how simple their problem is and how we dealt with it back in the day, brush our hands off, and be done with it, we could be right all day long. But wouldn't that be a one-sided, insensitive, oblivious conversation? Let's be honest: we probably do have great solutions to many of their challenges, as we have walked through many of them ourselves. We have similar stories with different names, but that is not the point. We want to listen and not do all the talking. I am learning that the answer to a lot of social challenges is the ability to listen and ask good questions. Sometimes you may even be able to round them up and point them in the direction you wish for them to go simply by allowing them to talk their way through your questions and come up with a really bright idea on their own. Yay, you!

Here are some questions for such conversations:

"How do you think that is going to work out?"

"Why do you think this happened?"

"How are you feeling about this whole thing?"

"What do you think they could have done differently?"

"Is there anything I can do to help make this better?"

Rule #4: Make Food

There is something about making homemade cookies or frozen pizza and boneless wings late at night that primes the teenager to hang out and talk. Many a self-quarantining, reclusive teen has been known to emerge from his dark room at the beckoning smell of nachos and wings. Food is a companion of conversation.

Rule #5: Be Available

I have heard it said that rules without relationship equals rebellion. I could not agree more, and in addition, I believe that without a relationship, no teenager will want to crack open his heart in conversation. Therefore, cancel some plans and do something fun with them, something that they want to do. Invest in them. Invest your time and money to have a relationship and the conversations will most likely follow.

Rule #6: Do Not Tell Their Secrets

If by some chance they tell you something personal, do not repeat it. If you tell all your friends and family in the name of a prayer request, you will lose the confidence of your teenager, and he will close up like a clam. Let him know that you are a vault, and the things he chooses to tell you are locked in.

Rule #7: Allow His Friends to Come Over

If you can create a place for his friends to hang out at your house, you have moved a step closer to real conversations. Let's say that being kind, hospitable, and friendly in the sight of your teenage son's friends is an advantage. And did I say that you should make food? Food for the win! Food helps people belong, and when they feel like they belong, they usually talk. When his friends leave, find something positive to say about them, and do not talk poorly of them. When you learn about your son's friends, you learn a little more about him.

Rule #8: Ask Your Boy for Advice

Tell him a challenge that you are facing at work or with the dishwasher or with your weight loss plan. Tell him a little piece of your heart and ask him what he thinks you should do. If at all possible, try to take his advice and report back to him with the results. Just creating some kind of open channel is a good start for a lot of moms who are trying to connect with their teenage boys.

Moms, don't forget to pick up your jaw. Carry on. You will most likely enjoy real conversations again one day, and I will bet that you will emerge from this season and be appreciated and valued. Just give it a little time and keep listening and making food.

> *Be quick to listen, slow to speak, and slow to get angry. (James 1:19 NLT)*

I started hiking with my boys as soon as they were old enough to ride in the baby backpack. The kind with the shade and little pockets on the side for juice and snacks; they had it made! As we walked and hiked together, we would gather rocks, leaves, acorns, and all kinds of treasures from nature. Over the years, we have continued to hike together, and I've found it to be a wonderful way to communicate with my boys. Something about the informal nature of walking outdoors next to each other lends itself to a more free-flowing conversation. Now that my boys are eighteen and fifteen, they are busy with school, work, and sports, but we still find time to connect on a hike, and I love it because that's when they open up to me. They share things they might not share if we were sitting properly at a table. Get outdoors and get your boys talking! P.S. It works on spouses too.

—Angela Richardson, @hookedonpink

CHAPTER SIXTEEN

Fire Pit Conversations

(When organized devotions were a disaster.)

A SHORT TRIP DOWN MEMORY LANE, AND IT IS ALMOST LIKE I AM THERE, in our living room with my parents, my two younger sisters, and my little brother as we sat in our PJs with clean, wet hair, attentively listening to my dad read from *Our Daily Bread* or a chapter from the Bible. We would each pray every night, oldest to youngest. I was always third, except for the nights where we mixed it up and got a little crazy and prayed youngest to oldest. Those were the nights that little Dave went first. In that case, I prayed fourth. We closed our family devotion time with a song each and every night. "God Is So Good" is the song I most remember singing. Sometimes we sang "Amazing Grace," and once in a while, Dad would play the guitar. If by chance we were driving home late, family prayer time would be had in the car on the way home. It was a steady, scheduled, and precious time growing up. It was so meaningful and so constant that I automatically thought that my future family would do the same thing when I was the mother.

My mom taught school before I was born, and after my little brother was in school, she resumed teaching. Mom is a naturally gifted teacher. She is organized and clutter-free. When we were little, she had charts for our chores and for the Bible verses we were learning. She had us create posters of our verses to be displayed on the refrigerator, and we got prizes for learning them perfectly in the King James translation. At the current time, my parents present a verse to their grandchildren each Thanksgiving or Christmas that we are all together. As each one, from the youngest to the oldest grandchild, says their verse, they get a twenty-dollar bill! This year, instead of giving presents, they awarded each grandchild one hundred dollars for saying their memory verse passage! (This is one of the many things I love about my parents.) Back to my mom. Did I say she was organized? And she loves to sing! So growing up we were a singing family. We sang in the car frequently. All six of us, in fact, were encouraged to sing as we harmonized Mom's favorite hymns. We sang all the Christian songs and "Do Your Ears Hang Low?" Our fifteen-hour car rides home for the holidays ensured that we would all sing, "Over the river and through the woods to Grandmother's house we go!"

Fast-forward to my reality. I tried. I will paint a picture for you of my attempts to have organized nightly family devotions. First of all, I am practically twitching just writing about it! The picture that first jumps to the forefront of my mind is that of the boys literally hanging upside down out of their chairs with an ADD-induced coma-like reaction. Their eyes were practically rolling into the backs of their heads as they asked, "Are we almost finished?" Back in the day, the boys fought a lot, so devotions were often met with scowls of sibling rivalry. There were feet in faces. There were clicking sounds and farts. But the bow on top of the whole package for me was when I asked them to sing a little song. I am not kidding you when I tell you that their brows furrowed, not with anger, but with complete, utter disbelief. Their mouths dropped open. "Why? Are you kidding me?" they muttered. Even Brian almost crawled under the chair at this point. Evidently, we were not a singing family.

Then there was the time I decided to make a Bible knowledge test to see what my boys actually knew about the characters and books of the Bible. I had such a great time thinking up entertaining questions about the disciples, the flood, the big fish, and the pit in Egypt. I felt like I had put my teacher hat back on. This was going to be so fun, and I was going to give an exciting prize! Fast-forward to the test results. My boys didn't seem to know Jack Squat about the Bible, and they couldn't remember the most elementary Bible stories. I was so upset! "Mom, why are you mad at us? We are so sorry. We just don't know the answers!" I could not imagine that I was such a failure. My kids couldn't remember that Noah built the ark. Are you serious? I practically ran to the local Christian bookstore and bought up all the little Arch books. (I am saving those, by the way, for my grandchildren!)

I remember several years later talking about the Rock of Ages, and to my dismay, my teenagers literally could only relate it to the Def Leppard song. They had not been exposed to the precious hymn referring to our Savior. The '80s band was their only point of reference. I felt like a terrible loser of a Christian mother. My husband was a pastor, and my own children did not know that Jesus was the original Rock of Ages!

Now, your kids might be more like my sister's kids. I once received a beautiful little bracelet from them. As I looked more closely, I realized that the artful piece of jewelry was actually made up of tiny safety pins. The pins had been individually beaded with several microscopic beads on each sharp pin. "Jesse and Katie made this for you," my sister said. "You have got to be kidding me!" I reacted. "You mean that they put these beads on these tiny sharp pins?" I was in disbelief and awe. Jesse was four and Katie was three. "Yes," she replied. What the heck?! As I wore the lovely piece, I could only envision what it would have looked like to have given my boys a box of beads and a pile of sharp safety pins! I swear to you that not only would no bracelet have been created, but they would have had a party sticking each other with the sharp points of the safety pins, and not only each other, but they would have pierced themselves for the fun of it! Blood and tears would have been my bracelet for sure.

In 2010, Brian was given a gift of something that is called life mapping. During two days we spent together in Colorado, with the help of a coach, Pete, the events of Brian's life were mapped out and written on large poster-sized sheets of paper all over the walls. Pete asked questions about Brian's childhood memories all the way up to his current happenings, and as Brian answered, occasionally referring a question to me, his past began to take shape, literally on the walls. The premise behind life mapping is that if you can actually see the patterns in which God has worked in your life from your earliest memories and you can be honest about what you love and what you are good at and what frustrates you, well, then you might be able to carve out what your future should look like. This was particularly helpful and freeing.

After the maps were drawn, Pete gave us an opportunity to describe things that were really bringing us satisfaction and things that were not really going so well. We thought a bit and shared how dismally horrible we were at family devotions. We felt so guilty that we could not get it together in the family prayer-and-Bible-reading department. After hearing our woes, Pete told us something that freed us up. He changed the way we approached Bible time with our boys. He said, "You guys aren't wired that way. You need to stop trying to force a scheduled prayer and devotion time because that is not really the way you do anything else. You need to build a fire." What? Why should we build a fire?

Pete went on to explain that people love to talk around a fire and that if we would build one and just be quiet, our boys would start to talk. They would talk about life, and we would get a chance to listen and hear their hearts, and at the right time, we would talk about God and his Word and how it had so much to do with what they were going through at the moment. So we did it! As soon as we got home from Colorado—I mean that very week—we went out and bought a little fire bowl. We put it in our driveway and set four chairs around it. We brought out some marshmallows and listened. You know what? Pete was right! What we experienced that night was so refreshing and real and not forced or awkward. We felt relieved. Maybe we were not the worst parents after all.

The fire pit is one of the best things we did to build communication with our boys; in fact, we are having one installed in our backyard next week with gravel around it, and I plan to string a few white lights on poles and throw some pillows out there. The fire, however, is a symbol to us of naturally occurring conversations. We do not always have to have a fire, but we do always have to pray and ask God for opportunities to point even our adult sons to truth and to God in a powerful and natural way. We don't want them to feel like they just check a box when they complete prayer times; we want them to experience life change and have an accurate view of God and his involvement in their personal lives.

Here is an example. When Zach was a sophomore in college, his spring break plans fell through, and he called Brian and said, "Dad, I wish we could just go to Florida and watch Spring Training." I have heard Brian say that if your college-age son wants to spend spring break with you, you should make time for him. So Brian took a few days off work and drove eight hours to Florida to watch baseball with Zach. They had a blast! They ate great food and watched their favorite team. One of the best parts, according to Brian, was that while he listened to almost sixteen hours of Zach's music in the car, they had incredible conversations about life. When they got back, Zach said, "Dad, I know you took off work and did a lot for me, and I just want to say thank you. It meant a lot."

Moms and dads, God has the ability to take the personalities in your specific family and bring you opportunities to have authentic conversations about God and the Bible in the context of events that are going on in your son's real life. I want to encourage you to pray and ask God for teachable moments, for naturally occurring situations where you have a connection and the chance to influence and share truth.

I still put verses on our fridge from time to time. We even had a little book of verses I taught the boys. Hiding God's Word in our hearts is powerful, but do not beat yourself up if your ways do not look like someone else's. God has given you everything you need to connect with your son. So if you think you are a bad mother, stop right now! Take what God gave you, and work with it, and make it amazing. If I had to choose between my boys being able to rattle off all the books of the Bible and sing the song of the names of the disciples and get every question right on their mother's homemade Bible test or having an accurate view of God and wanting to walk with him very authentically, well, I would have to choose the latter one. I am pretty sure that with your investments of time and your prayers behind the scenes, you will be surprised at the ways that God will draw your family into authentic prayers and meaningful conversations, maybe even with s'mores and a fire!

> *Teach them your word, which is truth. (John 17:17 NLT)*

When it comes to raising boys, oftentimes things happen that are beyond our control, and all we can do as moms is pray for them. What God has and is continuing to teach me is that prayer is the best option—not the last option. The same power that raised Jesus Christ from the grave is available to us (Eph. 1:17–23). That is a game changer. In other words, when we pray for our sons, we are accessing the heavenly Father, the creator of the universe. I love that Paul reminds us who the source of power is and how very powerful that source is. When we understand that, it changes our prayer posture to praying from a position of victory instead of defeat.

—Dawn Bloye

CHAPTER SEVENTEEN

Little Monsters That Drive People Insane

(The importance of training.)

"THANK YOU FOR THE DELICIOUS MEAL, MS. AMY. MAY I HELP YOU WITH the dishes?" That is a giveaway phrase—a total giveaway that someone has been trained. Young ladies who came to our house to spend time with our boys did not compliment the food and ask to help in the kitchen because they just enjoyed doing the dishes. They had been trained. They had mothers who had taught them to say that. Their mothers had spent time telling them what to say and why they should say it, and it spoke louder than the table conversations could speak.

I want to encourage you to train your son the same way. If you do not, he will probably drive you crazy, but he will most certainly drive everyone else crazy! Do you think that most runners just love to run? I doubt it. Do people working out in the gym have nothing else to do? No, they are busy. Are thoughtful, socially aware boys just born that way? No. People run and work out and train their sons because of the exponential results that will come from it. It is hard and it is inconvenient, but like training your body or your mind, training your son is remarkably important. No one else can go to the gym for you or run your calories off. Similarly, no one else is waiting to train the social awkwardness and naturally born selfishness out of your son. That is your job.

Be intentional. You may have to pause what you are doing or create teachable moments of practice, but training will pay off for you and for your boy. If you train him to be respectful and courteous, people will like him. He will have a head start in school, in the community, and in search of a job if he has been taught the necessary skills to thrive among people. Brian taught our boys how to firmly shake hands with a man and look him in the eye with confidence. When you teach confidence and social skills, you are doing him a favor and investing in his future.

We have always lived far away from my family, so our boys grew up talking on the phone to my parents. When they were little, I practically hovered over their discussions, teaching them not to dominate the conversation by talking about themselves the whole time. "Ask Grandma and Grandad what they did today," I would prompt. When they would finish the phone call and hang up, I would repeat the importance of asking people questions and helping people know that they are valued and that you do not just want to talk about yourself the whole time. That is training. Today, as adults, I overhear them ask, "How are you doing?" The blessing of intentional training at a young age is that it is soaked in quickly and comes out naturally in the future. You can train your boys to speak with confidence, pick up their messes, and be kind and patient. You can train them to be on time and work hard.

In an earlier chapter, I mentioned that I had read *Raising Faithful Kids in a Fast-Paced World* by Dr. Paul Faulkner. He and his wife, Gladys, interviewed thirty highly successful families and documented exactly what made them so successful in raising their kids. The Faulkners found that almost all thirty families said and did the same things. Remember? One of the commonalities was that all the parents were very intentional. Here are some of Faulkner's

findings: "The moms we interviewed were anything but unintentional. They worked at being great moms. They planned and set
goals—they were intentional."[1] Faulkner also comments that the
moms he interviewed "trained children for independence," "man-
aged discipline," and "insisted on high goals."[2] The book quotes
Danish philosopher Søren Kierkegaard:

> The loving mother teaches her child to walk alone. She is far
> enough from him so that she cannot actually support him,
> but she holds out her arms to him. She imitates his move-
> ments, and if he totters, she swiftly bends as if to seize him,
> so that the child might believe he is not walking alone. . . .
> And yet, she does more. Her face beckons like a reward, an
> encouragement. Thus, the child walks alone with his eyes
> fixed on his mother's face, not on the difficulties in his
> way. He supports himself by the arms that do not hold him,
> and constantly strives towards the refuge in his mother's
> embrace, little suspecting that in the very same moment
> that he is emphasizing his need of her, he is proving that
> he can do without her, because he is walking alone.[3]

As we are ultimately training our sons to walk alone, Faulkner
points out that the successful parents they interviewed were trained
for responsibility and leadership as well.

He tells of a young teenage girl who was responsible for budget-
ing and purchasing hundreds of dollars' worth of family groceries
each week. A sixteen-year-old boy was allowed to drive the family
pickup truck with their horse trailer and best horse to a vet in another
town. He explains that often parents wait until their children are
grown to give them big responsibilities, and by that time, they have
been held back and struggle to lead. "Our children, to be leaders,
ought to be out front, the first ones to do all the good and wholesome

things. If it is right and possible, why not? Encourage leadership at an early age," he suggests.[4]

I have seen some little monsters that drive people insane. Have you? Their parents want them to be free to express themselves. They want them to investigate and observe and come to correct conclusions on their own. They do not want to cramp the styles of these little guys; however, by not training them to do what is right and respected, they, in turn, hurt their boys. They hold them back because while their parents were waiting for them to investigate and observe, other boys were being trained to be leaders.

Parents, decide what is important to you and train your boys to do those things. Train them with skills that will benefit them in their teens and in their young adulthood. Let them get ahead because you trained them, and then you can reap the benefit of watching them lead confidently.

> *Children obey your parents because you belong to the Lord, for this is the right thing to do. (Ephesians 6:1 NLT)*

Never underestimate a boy. . . . He will literally look you in the face while he's doing something naughty and then grin and say, "I love you, Mommy!" True story! *Teach your boys manners from an early age.* They will always benefit from being polite and respectful. *Teach your boys to be leaders from an early age* so that they will be prepared to be the "man of the house" when the time comes. This is so important, especially in today's society. Remember that you're not just raising a son; you're raising someone's husband.

—Jenny Zacharewicz, mom of six boys (and
four girls) @bigfamilylittlefarmhouse

CHAPTER EIGHTEEN

Heroes
(Dad is more than a supporting role.)

THERE ARE THINGS IN LIFE THAT ONLY A MAN CAN IMPART TO A BOY. Only a man can transfer manhood, and only a man can model how to be a man. I am a believer in equality for women; we were created to be equal yet different. As a woman, I can lead with strength. I can make decisions and display independence, solidity, and vigor. There is something about raising boys, however, that I cannot put my finger on. When the boys were little, there were times that they just needed their dad. I could do the same things and say the same things and display just as much strength, but when Dad did it, they interpreted it differently. Dad had an air about him, and for some reason, the boys respected it and needed it. As a mom, I have to respect it too. It cannot hurt my feelings that sometimes my grown boys need to talk with their dad.

There comes a time in a little boy's life, in fact, that he must transfer his attachment from his mother to his dad. This is a healthy part of growing to be a man. I am learning that much of motherhood is actually about changing our roles to accommodate the needs of our growing boys. In the beginning, we actually carried them as a part of our bodies. We birthed them and nursed them and babied them. We protected them and cared for their every need. As they grow, we let them go little by little until they learn to be strong men without us. We will, in turn, love them more deeply by loving their wives if they are married, thus investing in their healthiness.

I asked Zach to share with me some things that stood out to him about growing up with Brian as a father. I told him that I wanted him to contribute to the thoughts in this chapter. Not one second passed before he began to pour out meaningful connections that Brian had made with him:

> Dad would create an atmosphere of openness, and his actions would communicate, "I am on your team." He would listen without reprimanding me, and now I realize just how rare that really is. Every son wants their dad to see them do well. Even today I asked Dad to come over and watch me hit the heavy bag, and I realize that I wanted him to see me do a great job, and he stopped what he was doing and came over to watch me. Dad has always been affirming. Every night he would tuck us in and tell us that we have what it takes. That built confidence in us not only to believe in ourselves but to know that we had a dad who believed in us as well, and that was enough right there. Dad shaped who we are now.

For the last twenty-six years, I have had a front-row seat to observe a great man in action as a father of boys. He calls them all the time, and sometimes I fuss at him for bugging our boys: "Brian, they are busy, and you just talked to them." He doesn't care. He calls them every day to check on them and to find out how he can pray for them. He encourages them. I am convinced that he is a big part of their lives because he pretty much knows what they are doing every day. He loves big, and he prays out loud for them every morning. He knew when they had tests at school and when they planned to ask a girl out. He was so involved in their lives that even when they were not at home, he would ask what they had eaten and would encourage them to order a big steak "on his card" if they had not eaten well enough! When they were little, Brian would wrestle them and teach them to play fight. He told them they were strong men. "Let me see those pipes," he would say, and they would flex their little muscles with grimacing faces.

One of our boys asked a girl to the school dance, and she said she would think about it and get back to him. Brian said, "What? She has to think about it? Well, you call her back and tell her that if she has to think about it, you don't want to go with her. You are too good for that." Brian instilled in our boys that they could pretty much do anything and that with a whole lot of prayer, God would open the doors to their success. Brian rolled down the windows in the car rider line at their elementary school and turned up their music. He yelled funny things out the windows, and although I'm certain he embarrassed them, he instilled in them an attitude of boldness and confidence while modeling humility.

One of the things I appreciate the most is that Brian taught the boys to respect their woman. "We don't hit our woman," he would instruct when they were little hitting toddlers. "We take care of our woman," he would model with a bouquet of flowers. "We protect our woman," he would admonish, even when he would have to come home in those early, early years to protect me from their disrespect. I was their woman too, and because of Brian's constant display of how to treat your woman, they are very protective of me.

Brian gave our boys a formal blessing on their thirteenth birthday. "The rights of passage have been reduced to drinking, driving, and sex," Dr. Paul Faulkner quotes Ellen Goodman, feminist columnist for the *Boston Globe*. He adds, "That is so sad. We need to make every good turning point in our children's lives a celebration. . . . The parents must back up their blessings with time and money and actions and efforts and prayer and praise and dreams."[1] Big dreams and big prayers. This is how Brian Bloye rolls, and it is contagious.

He celebrates the little wins and makes a big deal out of little deals, which makes us all feel like we are a big deal and we expect big wins. I am watching it work.

I will tell you a secret. Brian, though a strong personality and a driven leader, is, well, a softie. Every single time the boys were grounded, he shaved off a couple days of their time. If they had to come up with money, he chipped in. If he doesn't have something, he figures out how to make it happen. He is a cheerleader, a promoter, an agent, and a spiritual advisor. He has laid a foundation of the sweetest grace, and that foundation has been rock solid. He is our hero, and every boy deserves to have a man like this to follow. Moms, if your son does not have a man like this in his life, do not fret. Pray for God to provide role models, in various men, who will help your son develop into a godly man. Seek them out and ask them to invest in your son. God has an incredible ability to fill in the gaps.

When Dr. and Mrs. Faulkner wrote about the families they interviewed, they noted that the dads just could not wait to be with their kids. These dads made time to prioritize their families not out of a sense of duty but because of the pleasure they found in being home and investing in their children: "What every family craves from Dad is his simple presence."[2]

One of Brian's favorite words is *inspire*. A wooden plaque displays the word on a shelf in his office, a reminder to him to use his influence to love and motivate and to impart courage.

Dads, God has already set you up to be the hero in your home. Just be there. Give your time and attention and be a good listener. Your role is so valuable that God, the Father, shares his title with you. He is compassionate. He gives wisdom. He gives unconditional love. He provides security and forgiveness. He is accessible and he rewards his children. And you get the honor of imitating him! There is nothing that compares to the title of Dad.

> *As a father show compassion to his children, so the Lord shows compassion to those who fear him. (Psalm 103:13 NLT)*

Being a military wife and mom of two boys is a tiresome yet exciting adventure. We lived between a state of welcoming daddy home and telling him good-bye; the stress of managing everything in his absence produced a ripple effect on our boys. In these situations, I had a choice to make: Do I fill my speech with negativity and complaints or with excitement and anticipation of the next adventure God has for us? Let me encourage you, military mom, your response toward your spouse's deployments, changes of station, the new school, and the next house will greatly affect the type of man that your boy will become. Root your boys in the foundation of God's unchanging love, and he will carry them through your many military adventures.

—Kerry Mills, military mom

CHAPTER NINETEEN

Time to Paint!

(Alternating energetic and calm activities.)

LUCY MONTANA LOOKS LIKE A CHOCOLATE LAMB. SHE IS THE PUPPY I picked up when I flew to Montana. She is a beautiful joy, currently enduring a urinary tract infection, so she is peeing all over our house. This past weekend, I was up most of the night with said ten-week-old throwing up and peeing all over me and our bed and our couch. As we train her and love her and are completely exhausted by her, I am reminded of what it is like to have a little one in the house with lots of love and lots of needs. Could it be that Lucy Montana is contributing to this book about raising boys? I think so.

I have been reminded of the daily cycles that a new parent or veteran parent needs to maintain their own sanity. Brian and I did not let the sun set before we hastened to PetSmart and bought a plethora of canine survival supplies. I quickly learned that I needed a baby gate to bring up my labradoodle without losing my mind. She needed a crate and toys to chew and an antler, perhaps our greatest investment for this little, teething, sharklike, thrashing "lamb." This tiny antler stays on my nightstand as part of my morning routine. As Lucy waves her head in search of a finger to bite, we give her the antler. If ever the antler goes missing, I will cry tears.

I am finding that I have to create plans for this little puppy or she will run my day. I have to have crate time, antler time, run outside time, toy time. Similarly, young moms, if you don't plan your day and have a few activities in mind, your unplanned schedule and your boy will run your day for you. As they grow into men, they will slowly begin to make their own choices, but while they are toddlers and elementary age, you can deliberately make some choices for them that will help shape the way they think and develop their minds while saving yours. Even after elementary school, your influence in your own home can shape the way your sons grow and develop. Alternating energetic and calm activities will help you plan what is going to happen in your home rather than sitting back and watching what randomly unfolds.

"How fast can you run around the house?" Brian challenged. "When we pull into the driveway, let's see if you can run around the house four times!" Always up for adventure, Brian and I learned early on that boys must get their energy out. There are so many ways to help that happen. Here are a few random ideas.

Our boys could work up a sweat on our minitrampoline. Jumping at ten inches off the floor to their favorite songs, this yard sale find was a treasure.

In a quarantine attempt to unleash the energy of their little boys, mothers posted creative obstacle courses in their living rooms and hallways involving climbing over things and crawling under things. I saw brightly colored arrows made of tape to show the boys the way. Sliding and scooting and hopping on the path looked like such fun! My parents let us make forts with the cushions and pillows and blankets in our living room. We used flashlights and our imaginations to create adventurous spaces. Energy is sometimes released through intense creativity and planning.

Our swing set was a great investment, and climbing trees costs nothing at all. Bikes, skates, and skateboards (and helmets of course) were a constant companion of our garage clutter when the boys were growing up. And I think from age one to 101, boys will shoot hoops in the driveway! Have you heard of pickle ball? It is a cross between Ping-Pong and tennis, and it is historically an old person's game, but as of late, it has been resurrected as a valid youthful sport. Parks often have pickle ball courts, and we recently purchased paddles for everyone in the family. Parks are great, aren't they? Young boys and grown-up boys may love a new game to play outside. We bought a thirty-dollar badminton set for our backyard, and I am pretty sure the most fun had was in watching me fail at being able to hit the birdie.

Willard Harley, in his book *His Needs, Her Needs*, explains that one of the top needs of men is recreation. We can see that in the lives of boys, can't we? Often, however, women make fun of boys, and especially men, for having this need. We must realize that the need for recreation is God-given, and so as parents of boys, we will best serve them by creating opportunities for them to play hard.

As you transition from sweaty, energetic activities, have a plan up your sleeve, and if your boys are little, end the energetic competitions just before everyone gets overly tired and frustrated. Having a plan for a calm activity will hopefully help transition your rowdy group and give them something else to look forward to. Here are some ideas to trigger your own creativity.

Puzzles and board games and card games are quiet transition activities and can be left out as you continue working on them all week. Books, of course, are always a smart choice. Did you know that a person's overall academic achievement is directly related to their level of reading and vocabulary? Reading is totally underrated. I used to be a tutor in a children's reading club, and many of the boys in the club were not good readers. When they found a book that they were actually interested in, however, they were eager to learn. For example, if your son loves soccer, find a book for him about a great soccer player. If he loves fire trucks, order a book about fire trucks and visit the fire department. A little research on his favorite topics will make him a learner.

Most boys like building blocks and Legos. I always had a box of blocks ready with a building project idea that seemed to buy me a moment to get something accomplished and stimulate their creativity at the same time. Note that if your son is little, a project may only last five or ten minutes. Am I right? It is almost like you have to have your mental activity list ready or run a circuit of activities to keep them busy, happy, and learning.

Little boys can learn about the seasons by hiking and planting and working outside and getting dirty. They can get fit by doing jumping jacks and touching their toes and running in place. They can be big helpers around the house with pets and with learning to put away their toys. When all the toys are put away, it is time to paint. Finger paints and brush paints are a blast for little guys to be messy and creative at the same time. Don't underestimate the power of paint!

Now we must thank God for technology! I see tiny tots with their own devices watching movies and playing games. I think it is great in moderation—as long as it is an important part of the cycle of the day and does not become a babysitter or keep our sons from learning how to communicate by interacting with real people. I am quite sure we watched *The Sandlot* at least a thousand times.

One thing we seem to want to avoid at all costs is boredom. Parents do not want their boys to be bored, but I like this mindful quote from *More Than Happy: The Wisdom of Amish Parenting*: "Have the courage to allow your child to experience a little boredom from time to time. Then let them use their own creativity to amuse themselves. Try to create some 'white space' in a child's life instead of attempting to fill every minute."[1]

I could not agree more. In a society where every minute is accounted for, even our boys desperately need margin, the empty space. Like the edge of a page in a book, margin is something we must have in our lives. Can you visualize what this page would look like if it were completely filled to the edge with words? The last letters would be almost hanging off the page! That is what some of our lives look like, and that is the schedule that some of our boys are keeping. Wonderful things happen in the margins of our lives. Brad Lomenick, a leader at Catalyst, says this about margin in his blog: "Margin is a powerful concept. It creates opportunities. For businesses, margin is one of our top priorities. Margin in business creates profits. Margin in family creates memories. Margin in our personal finances creates generosity. Margin in our friendships creates significance and impact. Margin in our lives overall creates options. Options to pursue dreams, think, play, relax, meditate, process, grow and ultimately live life more fully."[2]

I am finding more and more that we are raising boys who do not know how to rest. If we can help them play well and rest well, then we will have done a great thing. Alternating energetic and calm activities might just make your day a bit easier. Remember to create a little margin for them and for yourself. You've got this!

> *For everything there is a season, a time for every activity under heaven. (Ecclesiastes 3:1 NLT)*

"Sink or Float" is one of my four-year-old's favorite calm activities when we need to sit at the counter or table or even on the floor. We fill one of my huge cooking pots with water, and he goes around the house and finds tons of random toys and items he wants to drop in the water. We make it a competition to guess and see who can get the most right on whether or not it will sink or float! It has helped him learn about density, and it's water, so it's so much fun! And it costs no money, which is a perk. Another calm idea using stuff around the house is to take a whisk from your kitchen and craft pom-pom balls if you have them, and you shove all the pom-poms inside the whisk and set a stopwatch or a timer. See how quickly he can get them all out using his fingers. Scavenger hunts are always a fun thing too, like "Find something blue or a book that starts with the letter M." He loves card games and board games. Pretty much anything you can turn into a "competition," and with a timer added, it instantly motivates him.

—Morgan Creed, entrepreneur
@shopremiridge,
mom of two boys

CHAPTER TWENTY

Dumb Men in Commercials

(Strong role models are crucial.)

"AMY LEEBO (MY MIDDLE NAME IS LEE), GET OVER HERE AND SHAKE that corn," I can hear my grandpa say. Grandpa had his popcorn maker, dripping with oil, plugged in in the living room and sitting on a stack of newspapers by his recliner. The popcorn kernels sat in a huge puddle of oil, and to keep it from burning, before it began to pop, it needed to be stirred or shaken. I was a child in the seventies, and we did not have microwave popcorn; I jumped up and shook that corn with all my might. "Amy Leebo, hop up and change the channel." We did not have remotes. We children were the remotes. I grabbed that large plastic knob and turned that channel. There were only about six channels. When you watched TV back then, you did not have the luxury of skipping the commercials, prerecording, or rewinding. You watched what was on and that was that. Today, we have the ability to skip over the commercials that waste our time. We jump right into the show, and we can even binge-watch our favorite shows for hours. I love the fast-forward button. It is almost like you can move through time and gain literal minutes for yourself. There is something of value, however, to the commercials we skip. Commercials give insight into our society and what we value as a community of people. They are the marketing tools that tell us who we are and what we want.

I have noticed that our most recent and now common commercials regularly depict men as idiots. It is the man who is completely clueless. His wife must show him how to fix it, how to find it. His kids teach him how to act and point out that he is simply incapable of the smallest tasks. The man has become used to his role in such commercials and is no longer surprised that he is a moron. Our commercial man shrugs his shoulders in submission and assumes the role of the completely ignorant, needy male. What does this say about our society? If you so much as google the topic of masculinity, a plethora of information and opinions will surface. Men are commonly deemed as violent, sexist, fragile, aggressive. Masculinity is misunderstood and devalued. This is sad and sickening to me, as men and women are totally equal, totally different, and both are vital. What would our society be without strong men who know what it means to be a man? It makes me want to shake the corn and change the channel.

"Maleness just happens.... Manhood does not," says Glen Stanton at Focus on the Family. "It must be created with significant intentionality.... Manhood is a behavior that must be taught ... an identity.... Manhood must be crafted."[1] I searched the internet to find a definition of manhood, but most of what described being a man was simply that which is the opposite of a woman. For example, men do not cry like women. Boys do not throw like girls. I am convinced that many boys do not know the definition of manhood. "No society has discovered any means of compensating for the absence of or poor quality of its men," Stanton suggests.[2] Might we look at the characteristics of a real man? Real men have self-control. They show respect, and they are willing to work, to provide, and to protect. They are loyal, humble, and compassionate. Real men are courageous, honest, and not passive. They step up. They have tenacity, and they display moral strength.

When our boys were little, Brian taught them an answer to the question, "What is a real man?" Having read *Raising a Modern-Day Knight,* Brian printed out the characteristics of a real man and posted them on the boys' bulletin boards. "What is a real man?" Brian would ask. The boys would quote from memory, "A real man is courageous. He is not passive. He waits for the greater reward. A real man has a work to do, a will to obey, and a woman to love."[3]

How does a boy, then, become a real man? The answer is simple. Hang out with one. In the fields, on the farm, on the court, in the city, in the school, and in the church, you will find real men. Being a real man, in fact, is contagious, and even though our TV may show us otherwise, I contend that our society is still full of amazing real men of courage and strength.

> *He who walks with wise men will be wise. (Proverbs 13:20 NLT)*

I am not sure words could do justice to the miracle God did when he put together the plan for my son, Collin's, adoption into our family. We were not looking to adopt, but a fifteen-year-old unwed mother that we did not know existed was choosing life for her unborn son and praying for the right family to adopt him. What seemed like a casual statement from a friend about thinking my family should adopt an unborn child she knew about turned our lives into utter chaos overnight. I had a daughter who was two years old and a sister growing up—I knew *nothing* about raising a baby boy! I had no desire to raise a boy, no nursery for a boy, and no idea what God was even thinking. I was terrified. I had no idea that eight weeks to the day after being asked the question, this precious son would be in my arms and that God in all his goodness and faithfulness would make not only the perfect place for a nursery in our home but the perfect place for my son in my heart. Raising my son Collin has been the gift that I never knew I needed. The love for our adopted son Collin is no less than for our biological daughter, Anna Kate. God has provided wisdom for every single day as the joy of experiencing all things boy has unfolded these last thirteen years. Trusting God was the key to the miracle of becoming a boy mom! Trust in the Lord with all your heart!

—Amy Barfield, adoptive mom

CHAPTER TWENTY-ONE

Sliding on the Bannister

(Stop caring about what everyone thinks.)

I WISH I COULD BOTTLE BRIAN'S LAUGH AND SELL IT FOR WHATEVER ails you. He is an overachiever and finds it difficult to actually relax, but he has become more intentional about rest and renewal. The boys and I grin when we hear him laughing, sitting in his recliner, phone in hand, watching random videos of a less-than-intelligent person doing something ridiculous, usually ending in pain! His laugh makes us laugh, a medicine of sorts. If watching crazy people catch fast-flying objects between their legs, jump off roofs, or attempt any obviously perilous pursuit is not enough, he then turns to the face-altering apps on the internet. You can make your face or anyone else's face bigger, smaller, older, or alien. This man has decorated all of us on his device and switched the faces of our families and friends on the face-swapper app, where someone's head has another person's face. We have been "put in" the aging booth, the clown booth, the "you are an inanimate object" booth, and the reverse time, "this is you as a baby" booth. Once, he even mixed Zach's face with a deer head on a wall, and the picture was a perfect blend of Zach with antlers! Brian is our family face-altering expert—he is the first to find any new app to make your day slightly hilarious.

The internet is just so useful, powerful, connecting, funny, and real. Well, some of it is fake, but people think it is real. Social media can call out to you and persuade you to put yourself in the "look at my perfect life" booth, the "I can spin all the plates and still look this good" booth. More than ever, we are beckoned to comparison and given a media measuring device that ensures that we will never measure up as individuals or as mothers. We innately absorb information and sort it out in our minds and hearts, and often it spins in our heads and returns to us as a threat or a reminder that we did not do enough. What will our boys become if they did not eat the organic food that the best mothers are feeding their babies? If we did not lose weight as fast as the girl posting her workouts in high speed on her Instagram, we might feel like we are not as beautiful. Does your dog have bad breath? Are your eyelids sagging? "Fix yourself and your boys and your marriage and your life, and prepare this perfect no-calorie yummy meal while you are at it!" the comparison trap mockingly calls out to us.

I will be transparent. Last night I was previewing a picture that is going on our family Christmas card, and at the last minute, I changed it and replaced it with a picture that makes me look thinner. I have been working really hard to eat healthy, and I want the more flattering picture. I think we all want to look good. We all want to be good parents, and we want to be spurred onward to good things, but get this: Comparison is a killer. It will snag you and make you hate yourself. It will rob you like a thief and make you lose your joy. Comparison will make you put pressure on your son. It will make you spend money you do not have, and it will wear you out!

I love Galatians 6:4. It says, "Pay careful attention to your own work, for then you will get the satisfaction of a job well done, and you won't need to compare yourself to anyone else."

Nehemiah was King Artaxerxes's cupbearer in Babylon, but he was burdened about his city, Jerusalem, for the walls had been torn down and the city was in disrepair from unrest. The king gave Nehemiah time off to go home and rebuild the walls of the city. It was a monumental task in and of itself. In addition, he had to lead a scared group of wounded people and rally the weakhearted and convince them that they could succeed in building a wall. I guess he was multitasked as an architect, builder, visionary, motivator, and protector. At one point in the story, the enemies are such a threat that Nehemiah and his people had to work and build while keeping their weapons at hand. They did not get to change clothes (sound familiar, moms?), as their work was exhausting and constantly under attack. Two specific men, Sanballat and Tobiah, sought to discourage Nehemiah and threaten him. (You must read the book of Nehemiah. It is a trip.) When these men constantly seek to distract him, Nehemiah sends this message to them, "I am engaged in a great work, so I can't come. Why should I stop working to come and meet with you?" (6:3).

Do you ever feel like Nehemiah? Can you relate to leading a ragtag group and doing a great work? When comparison summons me down from the wall, when the opinions and judgments of onlookers call out to me and naysayers bid me to stop my work to meet with them, may I be as focused and pointed as Nehemiah. I am confident in who God made me to be, and I am doing what God called me to do as I raise these boys. I am doing a great work, and I do not have time to climb down from where I have risen and meet with Comparison. We cannot descend to worry about what everyone thinks about our work. Can you imagine if Nehemiah had fallen to the discouraging threats and rationale of his enemies and friends? I am sure he had weaknesses and doubted himself, but if he had listened to the advice of onlookers who were not building a great wall, he would have never finished the project.

Nehemiah finished the wall in fifty-two days, by the way. I cannot imagine how he felt when the last stone was laid. He was a beast, and he single-mindedly led his people to fortify his beloved city. You are single-minded too, my friend. Sure, there are challenges all around that point their ugly fingers at you and make you feel incapable and inadequate, but you have been called to a great and high task, and like Nehemiah, you will do it and finish it if you don't come off your ladder of confidence in God and yourself.

The banister in our church atrium is smooth and descends so slowly that a young onlooker would be sure to think it a great ride. Such was true of my boys. When we first built our church, the atrium was hopping with people, and children were learning not to slide on the enticing banister. I do not remember exactly what was going through my mind at the time. I wanted to set an example as a leadership family that the banister would not be a playground. Certainly, an injury resulting from a fall would not be a good thing. At the same time, I did not want to set a tone of "Your dad is the pastor and people are looking at you, so stop." I always disliked that mentality, especially since my boys grew up in a fishbowl. I learned that no matter what you do, you will never please everyone, so stop trying to make everyone happy. Back to the banister. I told Zach not to slide anymore, as it was not safe or wise. Later, when no one was around, we helped him get in a good and safe inaugural slide, and he responded, "We don't care what anyone thinks, do we, Mom?" I knew he had heard that from me. We did not care what people thought! At least that is what I told myself and my children. His response prompted me to dissect exactly what I meant by that phrase. Obviously, we cared what people thought. We had moved across several states to reach the community by starting this church. This is what I came up with: we love people, and we serve people, but when we are doing what God has called us to do, we do not need to look to people for approval. *Approval.* I think that is a good word.

Young mom, older mom, tired mom, socially networked mom: you cannot do this parenting thing alone. Even Proverbs tells us to "cry out for insight and ask for understanding" (2:3 NLT). There is nothing that will replace the wisdom of those who have gone before you. We need mentors and friends along this pathway of parenting, as none of us have ever journeyed here before. None of us.

There is, however, a huge difference between getting good ideas, wisdom, and advice from smart sources and actually looking to be approved by or "liked" on social media or in our communities by our peers. You have what it takes to raise your boy—whether he goes to private school, public school, or home school; whether he eats McDonald's or carrots; whether he still has his pacifier at age three or not; whether you posted pictures of him on cute little blankets every four weeks or not. Maybe you buy your son a new car at age sixteen. Who cares? We could all learn a lesson from a great philosopher:

> *Today you are you! That is truer than true!*
> *There is no one alive who is you-er than you!*
> *Shout loud, "I am lucky to be what I am!*
> *Thank goodness I'm not just a clam or a ham!*
> *I am what I am!"*
> *That's a great thing to be!*
>
> —Dr. Seuss[1]

Stop caring about what everyone thinks! Do you.

> *Pay careful attention to your own work, for then you will get the satisfaction of a job well done, and you won't need to compare yourself to anyone else. (Galatians 6:4 NLT)*

Ever had a piece of parenting advice hit you square between the eyes? "Love the kid you have, not the one you thought you'd have" was the one that hit me. Whatever thoughts, expectations, and dreams we might have had before get set aside when we meet the kid that God gave us. Our kids may be completely different than we expected, but they are exactly the right kids for us. And we are exactly the right parents for them. When I'm wondering if I can be the parent my kiddo needs, I remind myself that I can. That child was handmade by God and handpicked for us. God, will for me, stretch me, and use me in the life of my child. And God will use my son in my life as well.

—Lori Wilhite, author of *Leading and Loving It*

CHAPTER TWENTY-TWO

Sometimes You Can't Fix It

(Pointing your son to God when your faith is small.)

PANAMA CITY BEACH WAS HOT AND HAPPENING. THE SMELL OF SUN-screen and the crash of the waves welcomed us to the Florida panhandle. The Redneck Riviera, as they call it, Panama City was one of the most popular of the beaches for Georgians, especially if you were on a little league baseball team. The beach town boasted seafood restaurants and putt-putt golf and many bargain beach stores, where we purchased Benny the Jet Rodriguez (an orange sand crab) and Z Diddy and Dr. Swag (two tiny turtles). We brought them home as prizes and little reminders of the joys of the beach trip. Notice I said trip, not vacation. There is a difference, you know. A vacation is where you relax and let your worries fly away; a trip, rather, is about going away but not vacationing. This was a trip, but we were excited about it. Taylor was going into the eighth grade, and his travel team, the Westside Warthogs, had an invitation to play baseball at the beach. So fun!

We amused ourselves at the beach in the morning and played baseball in the evening. Then we played baseball in the morning and hung out with the other players' families in the evening. The team won some and lost some, but overall, they were pretty good. I remember playing one of the morning games and breaking for lunch. Our family went to Quiznos for sandwiches and soup and returned a bit early to the field. Taylor was always very punctual—early, in fact, as this game was much more than a game to him. It was his greatest love and heartfelt dream—a dream to play in the pros. He was a naturally gifted player with obvious eye-hand coordination and a drive to hustle. He led by his actions, his goals, which were somewhat a secret in his own head with the questions of his success that lay alongside them. He was all heart, but he was shorter than the other boys.

The following year, when he started high school, he was five feet and one inch, weighing in at eighty-two pounds. I cannot tell you how many times he was given a kid's menu when we went out to eat. The last one he was given was when he was out with his friends at age fifteen. We remember these things and the sting that we felt each time. Once we took his girlfriend out to eat with us after an event, and the waitress gave her an adult glass and menu and brought Taylor a kid's menu with a Styrofoam cup and lid. This was painful for me to watch as a mother. Did these little waitresses not see that my kid was a teenager? He had more heart than anyone I had ever met. Countless times, he was told by other high school students to go across the parking lot to the elementary school.

Moms, I am going to share this with you because there is some-one out there who needs to hear it. I was often oblivious to the bullying that Taylor went through. Many years later, we are still in the dark as to the daily emotional beating that he endured. I am not saying that he was unliked. He was on the homecoming court every year and won prom king, but the things he dealt with because of his size are still unknown to me. It has fueled him and continues to fuel him. It has made him the person he is today, but I wish I could have understood a little more of what he was going through. Just because your son is well liked does not mean that he is not experiencing difficulty at school. Just look out for that; pray and ask questions.

Back to Panama City. When we returned early from Quiznos, our family sat quietly in the car; I guess we were all exhausted from the week. The team would have to play like World Series champs in order to pull off a win in this upcoming game. The playoffs were not promising at this point in the day. However, rest and hydration were the prescriptions for the lunch break, and with those, we could come back and win this thing! In our quiet moment in the car, Brian led us to heartfelt conversation as we all randomly and naturally talked about God and his care or lack of care about what concerns us. Did God care about baseball, our big dreams, the championship game? Suddenly, the game that our family loved came head-to-head with the deeper questions of our souls, and there was a hallowed moment in the car that afternoon that somehow, to all four of us, overshadowed the results of the game that lay ahead.

Now, we know that salvation is from God alone because of what Jesus did for us on the cross. All four of us have accepted his free gift of heaven, knowing it is not because of anything we could do. It is everything that Jesus has already done for us. We had settled that long ago. The question that day was this: Would we hold tightly with clenched fists the things we loved and desired the most, or could we release our desires to control our lives into the hands of the One who had the ability to make our lives work out? Did we really trust God with the people and things we loved and wanted the most?

"Pretend that there is a paper in front of you," Brian said. "The paper is a blank page of your life. Would you be willing to sign your name at the bottom of the paper with a yes even though you do not know what God may write on the paper?" Wow. That was a big ask for a middle schooler and his little brother. I wondered what the boys' reaction would be. Food for thought at least.

What happened next was one of my sweetest moments as a mother and, at the same time, a symbol of what would later become confounding bewilderment. Taylor, taking the initiative, began to pray the bravest, most heartfelt prayer, one that challenged me not only as a mom but as a follower of Jesus. Yes, he would sign his name boldly at the bottom of the page of his life and let God fill in all the blanks. He would do whatever God asked of him and trust him fully with all the plans and dreams of his heart. Zach agreed, and we as a family had symbolically notarized and nailed down our blank pages. Our futures were in good and capable hands. How could any mother ask for anything more? What a lunch break it had been.

Taylor ran out on the field, and I thought it was going to be a great game. But it was not. We lost. The postgame coaches' talk and the promise of the beach helped soothe the wound of losing, and it was not long until we found ourselves in the sand, the boys on their skim boards in the frothy shallow of the broken waves. We would make this a great night after all.

Within the hour, a skim board from another skim boarder on the beach flew out from under his feet and hit Taylor in the leg. We wound up at the urgent care for X-rays that determined that it was indeed broken. How could this be? What did he just "sign up" for? We felt like God was messing with him, but we chose to have faith and to acknowledge that bad things happen in this imperfect world.

In the weeks that followed, Taylor was on crutches, which preceded an orthopedic boot just in time for baseball tryouts for the new middle school team. Taylor was able to try out in his boot and make the team. Things were looking up! Now, for those of you who have boys in multiple sports, you know that there is a time when the sports overlap on the calendar. Just as we were finishing summer baseball and fall baseball tryouts, football had already started. Taylor was able to get the cast off his leg in time to start football, and after two weeks, we received a call that he had broken his collarbone in practice. The hit he received was so loud that the players heard it break and the coach called the ambulance. Now he was out for football and standing on the sidelines. What happened when he signed the blank page of his life with a yes to God?

I would like to tell you that that was the last of his injuries, but I will be honest and admit that it was the real beginning of many breaks and much inflammation and hope deferred many, many times since. Taylor went on to play independent professional baseball, but we are still waiting for big answers to big prayers, and I do not have an explanation. As I write this, he is six feet two inches and weighs 196 pounds, and the things he has been through have grown him in a way I would not have allowed if I were in charge. But I am not, and God is doing a thing. Taylor is still in the middle of a lot of waiting and working hard amid uncertain circumstances. God is making him a strong leader, and his future is bright.

I did not have the answers when Zach had a sport-ending back injury for almost two years. I took him to eighteen doctors and did everything we knew to do. I had to help him put on his socks. He had to carry a pillow to high school to sit on. We watched and prayed for what seemed like forever, and I did not know if he would ever recover.

I did not have the answers when Brian's dad, my father-in-law, drowned in a river when the boys were six and nine. Why did this happen? It was so unfair. I told the boys the only thing I knew to hold on to: God is faithful, and we can trust him. God knows something that we do not know.

As parents, we want to fix it, but sometimes we cannot. We feel helpless and trapped. You may be like several of my friends who have boys with far greater challenges that will never be fixed until heaven. You may have a son who is alienated from your family or a divorce situation that keeps you from being together. Sometimes as parents our faith is small. Sometimes we do not think that we can impart any explanation because we may not be sure we have enough faith ourselves. I have prayed, "God, you are on the line here! I have told my boys that they can trust you, and I need you to come through for them for the sake of your own reputation!" God is clearly on his own timeline when it comes to rescuing our sons from whatever it is that he is using in their lives. I heard someone say, "Expect that God is up to something good."

I want to encourage you that God is good, and he loves your son. He is so intricately involved in the details of his life, and he has plans that are good. When we feel weak and our faith is small, we do not have to know exactly what to say. Just point your son to Jesus and let him fix it or carry you and him and work behind the scenes the way he does.

What about you? Will you sign the blank page of your life with a yes? Will you let God write a story on your page? I find it is much easier to write a yes for myself than it is to sign up for a blank page for God to fill in for my boys. It makes me nervous. I do not know what he might do. But I will continue to expect that he is up to something good. Will you?

> *If I take the wings of the dawn, if I dwell in the remotest part of the sea, even there your hand will lead me, and your right hand will lay hold of me. (Psalm 139:9–10)*

"Where is my mom?" are the first words my sixteen-year-old son spoke seconds after suffering cardiac arrest. Good Samaritans had administered over one thousand compressions and one shock from an AED [automated external defibrillator] in order to resuscitate him. Now he was lying on a gurney and smiling up at me through an oxygen mask on the court where just eleven minutes earlier he had been playing in a basketball game. As this chaotic scene unfolded, I crumbled helplessly on the floor of that gym, screaming and crying out four similar words: "Where is my God?" My heart was instantly shattered, and my faith was overwhelmed. I couldn't fix it, and the heartache was unbearable. But God had another plan, and while his young life dangled between earth and heaven, God divinely orchestrated a vision (#JustKeepDribbling) for him to share through testimony that has ultimately increased the faith of not only our family but thousands: "And he that was dead sat up and began to speak. And he delivered him to his mother" (Luke 7:15).

—Jill Lentz

CHAPTER TWENTY-THREE

Do I Know You?

(Surviving middle school.)

WE STOOD WITH OUR FEET APART IN THE BACK OF A CATTLE TRUCK, holding on tightly and balancing with each bump in the dirt road. As we ascended the Guatemalan mountain, we witnessed the coffee farmers raking the fresh beans into perfect shapes as they dried in the arid sunshine. A motorcycle sped quickly past us on the one-lane road, and I let go of the sidebar of the truck just long enough to wipe the sweat that was running down my face. We smiled and said "Hola" as an old, wrinkled farmer with a donkey loaded with fresh sugarcane slowly descended on our path, a mental picture of the simplicity of the vintage mountain life. It would take the best part of an hour to arrive at our adopted and much-loved village of El Cimiento. When we reached our destination, a loud salutation filled the air as pressed faces on the school's windowpanes told us that our arrival was welcomed and anticipated. Despite the conditions, the thatched roofs, and bare feet, each and every face bore a genuine smile. The people of El Cimiento are dear to our hearts and are some of the most beautiful people I have seen. Of the children whose faces stayed with me in the pictures of my mind, the middle school boys' class marked a familiarity. Having taught seventh grade, I recognized the common traits of the middle school boy.

Each male middle schooler had his hair slicked with whatever gel was cool on the mountain. The golden-colored chains around their necks and glances at the girls told me that indeed the characteristics of middle school boys are universal. Smelling strongly of cologne, they laughed and looked at each other as if to be mischievous, all the while seeking approval, and I remembered just how much potential lies within each boy this age. Whether on a mountain in Guatemala or in your backyard, middle school boys will most likely bring out much fun and much frustration. They are changing and learning and figuring out exactly what kind of man they want to be. Raising them is not an easy job. Seriously, these years are not to be loathed or merely endured but to be treasured, as these boys, in between childhood and manhood, are figuring it all out outwardly and in front of us all.

Dr. James Dobson, who has excellent advice and has been a pillar of parenting wisdom through many decades, shares on his online site what perhaps is the best admonition for surviving this season of parenting. He says, "The most important thing you can do for your [son] is to just get [him] through it."[1]

There you go. Perhaps if you and he are still alive after the culmination of middle school parenting, then you will be deemed a success! If you truly can love and keep your cool without losing yourself, you can do anything, my friend. May Jesus be your helper. The end.

With that said, I will attempt to share with you some specifics that may encourage you on your journey. Middle school itself was difficult for both of my boys, especially sixth grade. Their hormones are just messing them up, and they are not quite themselves. I must admit that I can understand that much better now that I have experienced menopause! Sometimes you just can't help it. You need some grace, and I think they just need an extra dose of grace. OK, maybe a few extra doses. Dr. Dobson comes through with some more practical advice that I think is pivotal. He suggests, "The philosophy we applied with our teenagers (and you might try with yours) can be called 'loosen and tighten.' By this I mean we tried to loosen our grip on everything that had no lasting significance and tighten down on everything that did. We said yes whenever we possibly could to give support to the occasional no. And most important, we tried never to get too far away from our kids emotionally."[2] This is foundational. Major on the major things and let go of the little things. You will not be able to make a big deal out of everything and maintain a healthy relationship with your middle schooler. Perhaps the most valuable advice that Dr. Dobson shares with parents is this:

> To help you get through the turbulence of adolescence, you should:
>
> 1. Keep the schedule simple.
> 2. Get plenty of rest.
> 3. Eat nutritious meals.
> 4. Stay on your knees.

We certainly need a simplified plan for our own self-care in order to be our best selves during this season of parenting.[3]

Through my own journey of writing this book, I have recently read several chapters of a book that was suggested to me by a friend. *Mother and Son: The Respect Effect* has impacted the way that I want to communicate to my husband and grown boys. If I could have known its advice when my boys were in middle school, I think it would have saved me a lot of mistakes with the way I spoke to my sons. Author Emmerson Eggerichs says, "A woman responds to love. . . . A man responds to respect."[4] In fact, "74 percent would rather give up love if they could keep respect."[5] He goes on to say that "a teen boy needs to be respected,"[6] and a mother "need only say, 'I am not trying to show you disrespect when I confront your misbehavior.' Just using the word disrespect eases his stress. . . . Without respect a son reacts without love, and without love a mother reacts without respect. . . . Every mom can use Respect Talk. . . . This is the native tongue of a boy."[7]

I can think of times that I did not show respect even in the tone of my voice. I have a "voice" that the boys make fun of. I think it is the "I am trying to remain calm" voice. It is the voice I chose to use when I was trying not to freak out and scream, but it came across as belittling and condescending, and I still struggle to keep that "voice" of mine silenced in my times of controlled stress or anger. Do you have a "voice" that belittles or disrespects? I will bet that you, like me, are doing the best that you can and are not even aware of your disrespectfulness to your man child. This is a great admonition for all mothers of boys. They need for us to use the words "I really respect that about you." This is something we can all work on together.

I remember a feeling in the pit of my stomach when our home was filled with a foreign chaos, one that you could sense and almost touch. I can hear the words of a song I sang by myself out loud in the rooms of our house: "Oh Jesus come and walk the halls of this house. Yeah tread this place and turn it inside out with Your mercy. And Jesus teach us the prayers that open these doors. Until Your light floods in and illuminates these floors. And let Your truth be on our steps and in these rooms Jesus invade."[8] This song, "Invade" by Christy Nockels and Watermark, sustained me during moments of uncertainty as a parent. There were middle school parenting moments that had us baffled, and if you can relate to that, then you are not alone.

Yesterday I sat through two services at church. (I skipped the third one.) And if you want to count the practice run-through message that I heard Saturday night, then I heard the message three times. That is part of being a pastor's wife. I will be honest; there have been times that, during the third time of hearing the same message, I make my grocery list. But yesterday I listened again. I heard this message with middle school boy parenting in mind, and I had to apply its truth to this chapter because it is the best word I could give you. You are not fighting with each other.

You and your son or your spouse or the teacher or coach are not the problem. You see, there is a cosmic battle going on for the heart of your son. Evil has a strategy to stir up conflict in your house to distract you, disrupt you, divide you, and bring about chaos. We are fighting for the hearts of our boys, and we are fighting against spiritual realms.

Ephesians says, "For we are not fighting against flesh-and-blood enemies, but against evil rulers and authorities of the unseen world, against mighty powers in this dark world, and against evil spirits in the heavenly places" (6:12 NLT). Anyone who would dispute this has not raised a middle school–aged boy! Seriously, when the Bible tells us that our conflicts are spiritual matters, it does not leave us without hope or help. In the same chapter of Ephesians, we are encouraged to put on "the armor of God," which will help us "stand strong" as we fight for the hearts of our sons. Those pieces of armor include truth (We need truth in raising boys, right?), salvation, peace (Yes, please!), righteousness, faith, and the sword of God's Word. How can we win a war if we are in a civil war in our own home? Here are a few specifics for you to consider:

Do not yell and lose your cool. Middle school years led us to seek counseling. The best advice we received was not to power up. Do not try to match your son's intensity, because as soon as you do, you lose and wind up having to apologize. Brian felt the need to defend me sometimes and felt the need to power up, but we learned that remaining calm has lasting results.

Read the Bible and pray on your knees harder than you have prayed before for your son.

Do not be alone in parenting. Join a group of people who are in your same season of life.

Lay aside your pride and your need to be understood.

Major on the major things and let the little things go.

Remember that rules without relationship equal rebellion.

Be consistent. Lay out your expectations and the consequences for not following the rules. Enforce them consistently without being emotional or angry.

Have fun with your son, laugh, and make great memories.

The hair gel, the stifling cologne, the emotions all over the map—these will pass, and you, too, will survive middle school.

> *Let the peace that comes from Christ rule in your hearts. (Colossians 3:15 NLT)*

CHAPTER TWENTY-FOUR

You Are Basically a Taxi Driver

(Seasons of life and mothering.)

I BREATHED IN THE STEAM FROM THE HOT, MUCH-NEEDED SHOWER as I stuck my leg out of the shower curtain. Scrubbing the bubbles in my hair and balancing on one foot, I rocked the baby carrier with my other foot. As my infant screamed, I rinsed, rocked, and skipped shaving my legs. Would I ever be able to take a real shower again? By myself? I wanted to stay in there until I ran out of all the hot water. For those of you who can relate and are perhaps in the same stage, I want you to know that I have been taking showers by myself now for a couple decades. It happens. It really does! The season of tiny fingers sticking under the door when you are on the toilet and little voices that inquire, "When are you coming out?" will soon be in your distant past. Young mother, you are in a season that feels like it will last forever, but it is just that—only a fleeting season. Parenting, like life, is full of seasons, and the sooner we embrace the season we are in, the more contentment we will experience.

I figured it out. I did the math. When I could get my baby to drink whole milk and eat real food, I would save a fortune! The quicker I could potty train, the more I would save on my grocery bill. Just imagine what I could do with the diaper and wipes money. The formula alone was costly. And so it came to pass. The boys were potty trained and eating our food, drinking milk from the gallon, and just like that, I was in another season. Little did we expect that I would be spending my diaper money on t-ball. Next would come field trips and cleats and school fees and the middle school dance and prom and senior pictures and—what? College! Nothing prepared us for private college payments. It does not end, but it just gets sweeter. Life will hand us rehearsal dinners and grandchildren, and we will love each season!

When I think of seasons in my parenting, my brain recalls a specific smell—a stench, rather. If you are ever in the neighborhood football practice carpool, let me suggest that you race to sign up for hauling the boys *to* practice and never ever be the picker-upper *from* football. The sour smell of football pads will burn your nose in such a fashion that you may never recover. You will most likely roll down all the windows to keep yourself from heaving, as the stench will permanently mark itself on your brain. Seriously. Oh, what I would give to watch one of my boys play football this weekend. Stinky football pad season is real, but it flies by, I tell you.

We swore we would never be those parents who bought their son a car as soon as he turned sixteen, but when you have driven many a mile, year after year, and woken up at five-thirty every Saturday morning to drive your young son to travel baseball or band or soccer or whatever extracurricular travel activity he chose to participate in, chances are, when you see a little truck for sale on the side of the road near his sixteenth birthday, you might just sacrifice your own money to match his and buy that cute little truck and say, "Drive yourself to your many activities, and pick up your brother while you are at it!" Your taxi season may be over, but your season of praying harder for your adolescent driver will have just begun.

I heard someone say that you should not judge your parenting until your kids are thirty-five. Wow, that is a relief, right? Well, I think that is good advice. Until then, here are a few thoughts about the seasons of parenting your son.

Know your purpose and calling for your current season of parenting. Tom Patterson says, "Part of facing your future lies in recognizing the season of life in which you are living." There are things that I have time to do now that my boys are grown, things I did not have time to do when they were little. For example, I lead a retreat each year for ladies in ministry. I have been simmering on the thoughts and plans and prayers for this annual Cultivate retreat since my boys were little, but those were not the years to embark on such an adventure. Decide what is most important during your specific season and do those things. The season of life with toddlers may not be the season that you have perfect, clutter-free living room decor. You may not be able to do some of the things you are passionately created and gifted to do. It does not mean that you cannot do those things; it might just mean that you do not do them now. Know what you are supposed to do in your season, and do not feel guilty for not being able to say yes to everything. Another season is not far away.

Do not compare your season to someone else's season. It is easy to look at social media and think that you should be doing what someone else is able to enjoy in their season of impacting others. Remember that your season is valuable and fleeting. Don't rush it; savor it.

We can mourn the transition of our season, or we can embrace it and celebrate it. I have seen mothers crying as they send their babies to kindergarten. Now, tears may be customary, but do not weep that your babies are growing into another stage. It is healthy and normal for our boys to go to school. Their next step is crafted by God to be celebrated and acknowledged as a new and exciting season for you as well. Grab hold of it and make it great. Similarly, I have seen women who bemoan the idea that they are no longer in high school. The thought of being a grown woman is a downhill transition for them. If God has designed our seasons in life, then each season is valuable and precious. You are important as a mother, father, or grandparent, and God is not finished with you, so do not grieve or lament your past seasons; instead, we must clinch the season of our future selves and see all that we have been created to be. You have much to offer. You are gifted and strong, so step out with confidence and say it and do it and be brave with great expectations, because God has so much for you in the coming seasons of your precious life!

Seek support and wise counsel from people who have gone before you. It is fun to collaborate with friends who are in the same stage we are, but there is nothing that can replace years of experience.

Though we and our boys will grow and change, God will never change. He will go with you through each season of your parenting. Hebrews 13:8 tells us that "Jesus Christ is the same yesterday, today and forever." His Word is a sure, secure, and stabilizing force through all the seasons in which we find ourselves and each fresh season of our boys' lives.

As I am concluding this chapter, I am sitting with my husband by our fireplace. He is in his chair, working on his computer, and I am on the worn leather couch, pulled close to the soothing flames. It is a rainy Friday, and all that I hear is the cracking and popping of the fire. We have assigned our beloved dogs to their crates and are settling down for lunch by the warm hearth. The smell of pumpkin muffins in my oven has wafted into our living room, beckoning us to the kitchen. My house is quiet and peaceful. I am reminded that this, too, is a priceless stage. In fact, Brian built the fire over an hour ago, and as I labored in the kitchen, he called out to me and asked if I wanted to join him. The logs, turning to embers, are burning quickly and persuade me to savor them and the fleeting time I have with him by the fire. I will wait to clean the kitchen. I will stop the rush in my head that compels me to do more. I will sit and think and feel and take in this moment.

I am adjusting to this stage of quiet. It has not always been this way. From sleepless nights of infancy to toddler fingerprints and messes, my stages have changed from ball games and taxi driving to a semiempty nest. Each stage moves more quickly than the previous one. Now I want to be more kind and worry less, to listen more and be more content. I want to be in the moment with the people who are in that very moment. Life is so hurried, and like logs that turn to embers, we have this one precious life and one chance to love and savor each season.

> *Behold I will do something new, now it will spring forth; will you not be aware of it? I will even make a roadway in the wilderness, rivers in the desert. (Isaiah 43:19 NLT)*

When most people find out they're expecting their first baby, I daresay they don't foresee their future motherhood as a single parent. I'm venturing a guess that they dream about their future as a family unit consisting of a mom and dad, but sometimes life doesn't work out as planned. As a single mom to three teenage boys (yes, you read that right), my home is loud, rowdy, and at times, battling air quality control from dangerous odors of well-worn sports equipment. And there's nothing I would change. Becoming a single mom has been one of the best opportunities for my relationship with each of my boys. Do I want their parents' divorce to be part of their personal story? Absolutely not. My heart aches when I know the disappointment and hurt they've experienced. However, I also know that though I might be a single mom, I don't parent alone. If I trust God to take the heartache I've experienced and use it for his glory, then I also choose to trust he'll do the same in each of my sons' lives.

—Brandi Wilson, author of *Leading and Loving It*,
life coach @lovebrandiwilson

CHAPTER TWENTY-FIVE

I Did Spit on the Floor

(How to react to bad behavior.)

THEY TATTLED ON ME. THAT IS EXACTLY WHAT THEY DID. AS SOON AS Brian walked through the door, both of my boys spilled the details of the afternoon as though I were the child. "Mom spit on the floor!" they reported. I had never been previously accused of bad behavior by my own descendants. Brian, unbelieving and amused, sought to authenticate what he thought he heard: "You spit on the floor?" "Yes, I did," I admitted. I had hit an all-time low in parenting. I was so frustrated, I just had to spit. It had seemed to be the lesser evil option that must have run through my head in my moment of exasperation. I have no idea why I did it; I had never been a spitter before. I would certifiably put this in the drawer of my least proud maternal moments. Do you have any of these?

In this drawer lies another regrettable grievance, one that is often resurrected in conversation. I promise you that I was never one to use foul language; Brian often referred to me as "Polly Pure Bred," as I kept the rules and certainly refrained from swearing. This was until I became a mother of boys, and then one day it all piled up in the kitchen. I had reasonably dealt with the childhood fussing, the disobedience, the general lack of appreciation, but like a volcano that had smoldered and simmered for many years, I erupted. "I have had enough! D— it!" I wish I had a picture of the boys' faces, their open mouths, big-eyed stares as they literally slithered down the refrigerator side by side until they sat on the floor. "Did . . . did you just cuss at us?" one of them stuttered. "Yes, I did, and I might just do it again!" I retorted, somewhat glad that the shock had taken effect.

I had a small victory that day, as everyone toed the line. I was large and in charge, and you can imagine that instilled fear in my little boys. Who wanted to hear Mom spew out the profane *D* word again? Everyone would be on their best behavior that night. But I had unknowingly created something I would regret, something beyond laughable moments as young adults remembering the crazy stories of their childhood. I had opened a little can called "out of control," and I had spread it around my own kitchen.

When you spread "out of control," it lurks like a contagious virus, and you look back with regret that you ever let it out of the can, because it grows, takes on its own characteristics, and comes back to haunt you. Most of us have opened that little can in one way or another; fortunately, God has a way of redeeming misguided and regrettably opened cans. Here are a few thoughts on positively dealing with bad behavior without activating your salivary glands on the floor.

In keeping with our previously mentioned examples, let's first discuss the things we should not do as parents. I read an Amish parenting book many years ago, and a particular example stuck with me and impacted the way we chose to discipline our boys. The author wrote about a police officer, standing on top of a hill calling out to the speeding vehicles, "Stop right now! I'm telling you that you better slow down, or I am going to write you a ticket. Do not make me come down there!" Have you ever seen a police officer yelling speed warnings? Probably not. In the real world, police officers write tickets to drivers who speed. They are not typically emotional about it. "License and registration," they say. The consequence of going too fast results in a painful, expensive, yet nonthreatening little ticket. Usually it makes us want to drive slowly. Parenting is similar, isn't it? It is indeed the real world for which we are preparing our sons, so like the real world teaches us, we do not have to threaten and warn about what we might do. We do not have to tell them to wait for Dad to get home. We do not even have to repeat all the imminent consequences. On the contrary, we must do the nonemotional, non-threatening thing that we previously stated that we would do, and they will eventually learn, like most drivers do, that we mean what we say and are not going to get all worked up about it.

Do not count. "One. Two. Don't make me say three!" How many parents have you heard threatening their little guys with numbers? Boys are smart, and they know which number makes us do what we say we are going to do. Leave the numbers to *Sesame Street* and stop the threats. Only promise consequences that you are actually willing to carry out.

Do not power up. A friend of ours once told us that we needed to be stronger willed and more powerful than our strong-willed son. We needed to top his stubbornness and aggression by matching his intensity. Now, for some of you who have compliant boys, that could be a good piece of advice, but if your son is over-the-top strong willed, it will make you a very stubborn, loud, unattractive mother. I found that it was too much to top his behavior. I was so exhausted and ugly by the end of the day, and I felt like I had been pinned in a wrestling match and just wanted to tap out.

So what are some things that might work for you? Be consistent and keep your promises. Your son should know that you will do what you say. Be willing to inconvenience yourself. If you say that you will lose a play day, then you will have to lose it. It is difficult to get up off the couch and discipline a child, but if you do not, you will still be sitting there a decade later when the stakes are much higher.

One of the things that worked for us as we tackled poor behavior was taking away their favorite things. For young boys, it may be a game or TV or a favorite snack or dessert. For older boys, it may be a cell phone or a social event. Once, we took most of the things out of one of our boy's rooms, and Brian took the door off the hinges. He was left with only his basic needs. I think that taking things away is effective if it is for a short time. Parents who take things away for a month or more usually wind up punishing themselves and frustrating their son. A few days or maybe a week is a big deal to a kid.

I remember the last time the boys fought. Taylor was in high school and Zach was in middle school. Brian told them that if they ever fought again, they would miss their game. As athletes, that was a big, big deal. Somehow, they got into it, and sure enough, Brian called Taylor's baseball coach and Zach's football coach and told them that the boys would be missing a game. We did not know what to expect from the coaches, but both of them respected Brian's decision. Brian told the boys to pack a suitcase and get in the car. (I think they thought they were going to the detention center, as Brian had previously taken one of them on a purposeful tour.) They wound up, however, in a cabin in the mountains, fishing and talking. As they were casting their lines in the river, Zach commented, "I don't know a lot about parenting, Dad, but you make us miss our game and take us fishing. This doesn't make any sense to me." Brian explained that they needed time away together to talk about what was important and what kind of men they wanted to be. Dads, one of the best things you can do is spend time with your son. The moment our boys began to act badly, Brian would jump in and invest more time in them. We almost always saw an immediate response.

There are so many things I would do differently if I could go back and do it all over again, especially with Taylor, our oldest. You know the first child is basically an experiment! As new parents, we were surprised that at six months old, he scooted in his wheeled seat to our potted ficus tree in the living room. His little hand began scooping out dirt and throwing it on our light-blue carpet. "No!" we warned. "That is a no-no!" As new parents, we laughed out loud as we told him over and over and moved his little wheeled scooter. He continued to scoop the dirt, this time looking right at us as he did it! We should have known then that he was a strong one.

I have left many grocery carts full of groceries in the store, unable to check out because of extreme behavior. At seven and a half months, yet unable to walk, Taylor would no longer be contained by his crib. He pulled himself up and jumped until he could hoist himself over the top rail and land on the floor in a heap. We could hear this from our bedroom, and after several nights, we were afraid that he was going to hurt himself, so we bought him a toddler bed at eight months old. A couple months later, he threw his bottle across the living room. He was finished with baby stuff. One of his first words was "Myself!" He wanted to do everything by himself without our help. He taught himself how to ride a bike because he did not want to wait until Dad got home. He pulled all of his own teeth. He was incredibly sweet, but he threw fits multiple times a day. I thought I was going to go crazy! I would often in frustration call Brian at work, not knowing what to do with this wild boy. He would gently remind me that I am the mother. Sometimes I felt like Taylor was in charge. After all, when he was two, he told us, with his little finger pointing at us, that we were not in charge and that he was in charge. Maybe I believed him. At eighteen months old, he unbuckled himself from his seat belt as we drove down the highway. I prayed that he would not open the door.

Proverbs 22:6 tells us to "train up a child in the way he should go; and when he is old, he will not depart from it." I guess that we can examine that verse and put it up against all the people we have ever met and decide what it does not mean. It could not mean that if you are a good parent and train your son the right way, then he will always do the right thing and not depart from what you told him to do. We have seen that this is not always the case. So what does it mean? The phrase "in the way he should go" actually means "in his way," and it is referring to the way God wired him in his creation. It means that we, as parents, must find out how our boys are wired, what their personalities are like, what they are good at, what frustrates them. We must parent them with those things in mind. Study your son and know how he thinks and ask God to help you train him "in his way."

To the parents of the strong-willed boy, I want you to know that you are going to make it. I prayed for world changers, strong leaders. I just did not know that world changers come into the world really raw, and it takes a lot of prayer and God's grace to take a rough little guy and watch him become an amazing warrior and a great man. My sons are both great men, and we do not attribute that to our parenting. I am very humbled that God has taken their strong personalities and made them into great leaders. It is overwhelming.

Mom, the days may seem so long, and you may not feel like you are making a difference, but hang in there, because just when you feel like your house is at its chaotic height, a great young man is being developed. Be consistent. Be loving and patient and kind, and try not to spit on the floor!

> *The Lord is righteous in all his ways and kind in all his deeds. (Psalm 145:17)*

God is the perfect parent, and yet his kids can be terrible. That gives me comfort because if the perfect heavenly Father has children that struggle, then who am I, in my very imperfect parenting, to think mine won't?

—Carla Davis

CHAPTER TWENTY-SIX

You Have Baggage

(Figuring out your dysfunction so you don't pass it on.)

MY GRANNY LIVED IN A CHICKEN COOP. SHE MARRIED MY GRANDPA AT age sixteen and moved from North Carolina to the Texas oilfields before the big oil was discovered. Grandpa was in "the service," and as a military family of four, they found a renovated chicken coop to rent. Granny had my uncle Roger at age seventeen and my dad at age nineteen. When they moved closer to home, they had an outhouse until my dad was in first grade. My grandpa, in his youthful days, had been a slop boy, pulling a cart and picking up slop from all his neighbors to feed his pigs. There was a lot of love there, as my granny was one of the biggest, smallest prayer warriors I have ever known. There was also a lot of unhealthiness, and the fact that my dad has a PhD in counseling is a huge achievement.

On my mother's side, my great-grandfather lost his job during the Depression, and my grandma was the only one in the family who could find work. She had to quit high school her senior year to work in a mill to be the breadwinner for her parents and her four younger siblings. She met a handsome supervisor at the mill and eloped at age nineteen. Her dad was very concerned that their family would not have any money, but her husband, my sweet grandpa, sent every cent of her income home to her family until the Depression was over.

He had been the second youngest, with six older sisters and one younger sister. He was born in 1903 and graduated from business college in 1922. I remember hearing stories of how his dad was a chicken farmer, yet they were not allowed to eat the eggs. They were the only house around with electricity, one lightbulb that they were not allowed to use. Grandpa got a weekly bath in the tub of water that had been previously used by all six older sisters, as they took baths by order of age. Think about that. He always got the chicken butt at mealtime. He was a hard worker and one of the best people I knew. The precious heritage of love and hard work has been passed down to me, yet the threads of unhealthiness have also run through our family lineage.

When you are growing up, you get what you get—all of the good and all of the bad. You do not get to choose your family or the baggage they will pass to you. You can, however, control what you do for yourself and your son. You can fix a lot of what was broken. I have heard it said that "you may have Jesus in your heart, but you have Grandpa in your bones!" That is a funny but accurate statement. The blood in your veins is from your mother and your father. They most likely passed on to you a set of wonderful qualities and characteristics, but somewhere there is a bit of baggage. Sometimes it is obvious, and people talk and laugh about it, and sometimes it is not so clearly defined. It may take you years to discover it.

Picture a lovely bride on her wedding day. She has adorned herself with the most beautiful gown. Her hair is flawless, and her skin is glowing. The couple anticipates a happy, loving life together. Can you imagine how amusing it would be if the bride walked down the aisle with a couple suitcases? Maybe even a travel bag or a backpack. As funny as this picture may seem, the truth is that we all walk down the aisle with invisible baggage. We will potentially carry it right into our marriages and into our parenting. I have heard it said that what we don't repair, we repeat.

The Adult Children of Alcoholics Syndrome is an interesting book written by Wayne Kritsberg. It specifically addresses alcoholism, but I believe many of the principles are true for other situations as well. Kritsberg says that "the alcoholic system will recreate itself generation after generation if the family is not treated. . . . A great number of adult children of alcoholics come from families where there is no alcoholic drinking taking place. If alcoholism is in their family history, they will have Adult Children of Alcoholics Syndrome."[1]

It is so important to admit that we have a bit of dysfunction and to move toward healthiness. If we do not, we may unintentionally pass our dysfunction to our boys. Brian and I have made it a practice to pray specifically against generational baggage, sins that were somehow passed down from generations and things that have potentially kept people in bondage for many years. We ask God to show us things that we cannot see, and we pray for a breakthrough for us and both of our sons.

What should we do to identify our own baggage and keep from passing it on? Here are a few thoughts.

Seek Counseling

I have mentioned that Brian and I have a counselor. We have been there several times to just talk about life and things that we are dealing with together. It is amazing how counselors have been trained to ask certain questions to trigger your thoughts and your memory. You may not realize why you do certain things that you do, but a Christian counselor can help you see your responses in light of the experiences that you have had and help you. Honestly, as I have struggled with feelings of not being enough or doing enough, I was sure I would not pass that down, but like a slippery hand that could not hold on, the control I thought I had was not enough to protect me from unintentionally passing my baggage to my boys. I see them deal with things that I see in myself. What we can impart to our boys is an understanding that we all have stuff to deal with and a desire to walk in freedom. We need advice and wisdom, and we cannot figure all this stuff out on our own—we are too much in the middle of it. Consider finding a Christian counselor and start moving toward healthiness.

Be Honest

It has been a painful experience for me to be honest about myself and my shortcomings, especially when I am trying so hard to do everything right. It is also very difficult to admit that my own original family has flaws. Here is what I have learned. When we can admit that people were not perfect in the past, it does not mean that we are being unfaithful to them or turning our backs on those we love. In fact, the ability to see imperfection in ourselves and in those we love moves us toward wholeness and helps us love bigger. All of us are flawed, and all of us can grow in love and healthiness when we are willing to take an honest deeper look.

Forgive

You cannot move forward in healthiness if you do not decide to forgive those who knowingly or unknowingly have hurt you or those you love. The Bible speaks of unforgiveness as being a "bitter root." I have heard that verse interpreted as a reference to a root that was used for dyeing cloth. Like the stain of the root, bitterness will color your world and the way you look at it. Take the root of bitterness out of your life so that you can see clearly.

Do Not Beat Yourself Up

When I think of my impatience as a young mother, the thoughtless comments I have made, the stress I often still exude in my home, I am tempted to feel like a failure. The enemy would love for me to think that I have messed up my boys and I am a terrible mother, but I will choose to believe the truth. I am a great mom, and although I am not perfect, I have decided to hang out in the realm of humility and healthiness as I continue to grow and love more deeply and with greater understanding. Choose truth and give yourself a break. You are probably doing the best you can.

Realize That Your Son Will Have Baggage

We live in an imperfect and fallen world, and there is nothing we can do to shield our sweet babies from everything that life, experiences, love, hurt, and family lineage will impart to them. Their life has been handed to them, and as we give them the proper tools, they will learn to carve out a healthy path. Both of my sons have grown up as pastor's sons in a large church. They have lived in a fishbowl. It is a good and wonderful fishbowl, but there are challenges that come with it. I cannot change that for them, nor would I want to. It is their life. I can however be honest about my shortcomings and continue to point them to Jesus, who is the ultimate Counselor.

As we seek to identify our baggage and move toward healthiness, it is a comfort to know that God is tender with us. He is moving on behalf of our boys with all their best interests in mind. He constantly works behind the scenes, and his mercies are new every morning!

> *The faithful love of the Lord never ends! His mercies never cease. Great is his faithfulness; his mercies begin afresh each morning. (Lamentations 3:22–23)*

I'm Jenniffer, married thirty years with a twenty-five-year-old son and twenty-three-year-old daughter. I come from quite the dysfunctional background, and what I've learned very early on is ... the cycle must be broken! My years before walking with Christ, well, let's just say I was on the hamster wheel of dysfunction and destruction. So when I met and married my hubby, those ten trailers of my baggage to his one, LOL, definitely began to play out their effects. It was quite the rocky road. Imagine this ... wedding dance ... fight, honeymoon ... bigger fight, plane ride home after being married for less than a couple of weeks ... already thinking of divorce and why did we marry one another? Oh my goodness! As a result, he and I made the best decision ever and went to Christian counseling for several years. Though we're nowhere near perfect, we have fought tears, blood (not really, but it felt like it), and sweat to not only better our relationship and have a sweeter intimacy with Jesus but also prevent our kids from continuing the cycle of pain, abandonment, and so many negative things that could have been inadvertently heaped onto their backs and passed on to future generations. Through the promises of God's Word as our backbone, and purposely placing him as numero uno in our family, and the counseling, we firmly believe our kids have been delivered from any past cycles. So my biggest advice, as difficult as it can be, is better look inside yourself, really stare at yourself in a mirror and ask the Holy Spirit to guide you as to what needs to be sifted and refined within and *go* to Christian counseling. It's something you'll never regret. So I'll end with this: we've always told our kids, if we're fortunate enough, we'll pay for your undergrad and your counseling one day, LOL, because we have never claimed to have figured it out or be perfect parents. We know mistakes were made. We just had, and have, a lot of love for them, and we rest in the fact that we did the best we could. Presently, my husband and I still pop in to counseling every year, for what we call tune-ups. You wouldn't let your cars continue to drive and function well without caring for them, right? So with what's most precious, marriage and family, we must care and tune those up as well.

—Jenniffer Marblestone, flight attendant

CHAPTER TWENTY-SEVEN

The First Five Minutes

(Mom sets the tone.)

HAVE YOU EVER NOTICED THAT THE FIRST FIVE MINUTES OF ALMOST anything set the tone? The first five minutes of a blind date can set the tone for the whole evening. The first five minutes of a movie or concert can generate an opinion and capture your interest in a very short period of time. In the first five minutes of a speech, you generally decide if you like it or not. The first five minutes of a ball game set a tone of momentum and often can give one team an advantage.

I remember taking piano lessons my senior year in high school. My sister and I went to our first lesson together, and something cracked us up. We laughed so hard that we almost fell off the piano bench. We could not get ourselves together! The one who sat at the piano tried not to laugh, and the other who was waiting her turn sat on the couch and was determined to squelch any possible giggle. The first five minutes set the tone for not only that lesson but each lesson that followed, for every week yielded another challenge of uncontrolled laughing. We would pep talk ourselves about the seriousness of learning our instrument and valuing the money our parents were spending on lessons. We would bite our lips and cover our mouths, but we could not stop. We laughed and laughed until we finally had to stop taking lessons from poor Mr. Jim, who could not teach us one note on that piano!

Similarly, mothers have the unique God-given ability to set a lasting tone in the home. It is our honor and our responsibility. I have noticed that the first five minutes usually set the tone for the evening. When your son comes home from school, a warm, happy welcome will go a long way. An offered snack and a few questions about his day can make him feel like home is happy. He will usually go his own way to play or do homework or watch TV, but the tone has been set, and the mood of the evening will most likely follow that tone. When we set tones of frustration (which I have been known to do), we will create an unsettled feeling in our home, and it too will permeate the air for probably the remainder of the evening.

Often it is up to us. I do not know why, but I know it is usually true. The old saying goes "If Momma ain't happy, ain't nobody happy." The opposite is true as well. If Mama is happy, then she sets a happy, peaceful tone in her home.

Between writing the previous paragraph and this one, I paused to put dinner in the oven, and my new puppy created a puddle on the floor that must have been bigger than she is. Considering the fact that I have cleaned many various and similar puddles today, I became frustrated. Simultaneously, I heard the garage door open, signaling that Brian was home from work. I thought about what I had been writing and decided to make the first five minutes the cheeriest minutes of my day and his. I chose to smile big and give a big hug when, in fact, I wanted to vent about the continuous puppy puddles. I promise you, as I threw my arms around this man, he said, "It makes me so happy to see you with a big smile." (I did not have a big smile yesterday.) He grabbed a snack, and as I threw dinner in a pan, he sat down to watch a minute of *Behind the Music* with Tom Petty. Boom. Five minutes. It was an internal fight for me, and I do not know why it is often that way. I expect that our tone-setting ability is such a precious gift from God to our families that the enemy would wish to tank it each and every day.

Moms are agents of hope, and the tone we set can actually impart hope to our boys. Psalm 71:5 states, "O Lord, you alone are my hope. I've trusted you, O Lord from childhood." Chuck Swindoll encourages us with this definition: "Hope is a strong, confident expectation in God's future faithfulness and his presence."[1]

In times of uncertainty, how incredible that we can set a tone of hope in our own homes and invest in our sons who will one day be able to say that God has been their hope since their childhood.

Moms are also agents of peace, and our homes are a refuge where our sons can be themselves. They can relax if we set a peaceful tone. The world may knock them down or bully them or stress them out, but at home, there is peace. How beautiful that we can invest so powerfully in their emotional well-being.

Rather than setting tones of comparison, critique, depression, guilt, laziness, fear, or anxiety, may we be moms who embrace and transfer tones of the fruits of the Spirit. The list of these God-produced qualities is in Galatians 5:22: "But the Holy Spirit produces this kind of fruit in our lives: love, joy, peace, patience, kindness, goodness, faithfulness, gentleness, and self-control." How can we do this on our own? We cannot. We do not muster up grit to display this kind of behavior. Notice that the verse says that "the Holy Spirit produces this kind of fruit."

In the Old Testament, God is often referred to as El Gabor. This name means that God is a warrior. He fought for his people, and he displayed uncommon strength. Mom, God will be your El Gabor. He will fight for you in your attempts to set positive tones in your home when you feel like you are running on empty. El Gabor will rescue you and enable you to fill others with hope and peace when you do not have much hope or peace to impart.

Hook up to his power. Draw near to him and let his Word soothe you and give you everything you need to exude those attractive fruits of his Spirit. When we concentrate on those first five minutes, the rest of the morning or evening will most likely follow in the tone we have set. You are a tone setter, and your son is going to love growing up in your home because of it!

> *It is better to live alone in the corner of an attic than with a quarrelsome wife in a lovely home. (Proverbs 21:9)*

The journey of raising our son with significant special needs has been fueled by hope. When our world collapsed at the news that Damian experienced a global brain injury at birth, I had no idea that we would need the hope that only God gives. Hope was a gift at that very moment and continues to be today. Our amazing son is a teenager now, and over the years I fought for inclusion and celebrated his breakthroughs in learning. I comforted him as he courageously endured numerous surgeries, hospitalizations, and medical procedures. I encouraged his tenacity to learn music, ride a horse and a bike, play in a baseball league, and perform in concerts and plays. I am grateful to God to be his mom and long for him to live a full life filled with love, joy, laughter, and hope.

—Dr. Zarat Boyd

CHAPTER TWENTY-EIGHT

My Brother, Camo, and Military History

(Training your son in the unique way God made him.)

I ALWAYS WANTED A BROTHER BECAUSE I WANTED SOMEONE TO PLAY fight with. My two little sisters were much smaller, and I thought it would be fun to have a rambunctious little sibling. When I was almost eleven, the school bus brought us girls home one warm February day in South Florida, and Dad met us in the front yard. "You have a little brother!" he exclaimed. We could not have been more excited. I remember the very day that I last beat him in arm wrestling with my left arm. (He could beat me in every other contest, but I held strong on the left arm until he was in middle school!) The age gap between us meant that I was away for most of my brother's growing-up years. I regrettably missed a lot of soccer games and birthdays and dates and school programs. I missed watching TV and popping popcorn on the weekends. Most of our lives, we have lived far away from each other. When I came home from college and Dave and I hung out, people often thought I was his mother. One thing I remember about Dave growing up is that he loved to wear camouflage and loved the military. How fitting, as he is currently a colonel in the United States Air Force! Dave is a man's man. He knows what he wants, and he goes for it. I love that about him.

Today I called my parents and asked them questions about raising my little brother (with three older sisters). It was fun to hear them describe Dave as a child who knew exactly what he wanted to become. Dave set the scene outdoors for his plastic toy soldiers. Clothed in his usual camouflage, he melted into the scene as he constructed a set in the yard with bricks. He masterfully built walls, mounds, and hills of dirt, preparing the battlegrounds for his miniature fighters. I recall that Dave read thick books about military history (in which he later earned a master's degree). The books were mostly stories of the lives of great men and how they conquered fear. It became one of Dave's goals to continuously move out of his own comfort zone in order to develop greatness and push himself toward his dreams.

As I listened to my parents tell of his adventures, I could feel their joy and pride in him, even as a little boy. They could see who he wanted to be, and they did something powerful. They cultivated his dream. I asked how they supported his goals, and my mom replied, "I just enjoyed it." I think they just sat back, as parents must do with their fourth child, and watched him play and read and become the man he wanted to be. They tilled the soil of his heart and mind and celebrated him.

Dave recalls a strategy in his blog posts at alphatangocounseling .org. His writings, entitled "200 Words or Less," are directed to men. In "Where's the Incentive?" he tells of a motivator that he himself has copied from our parents. Dad and Mom paid Dave to read books about great men and great faith. Dad picked the books he thought would shape the values of his son while supporting his dreams and goals. Dave has since found it to be resourceful in his own parenting. Here is what he has to say:

Kids respond well to incentives. We all do actually. I go to work every day because they incentivize it with money. I don't drive 100 mph because they'd take my money away. A basic principle of economics is that our behavior is shaped by incentives and disincentives.

As parents, we need to fully leverage this principle to our advantage. Some parents pay their kids an allowance to do chores or mow the lawn. But is that truly what you desire them to do? They'll become adults who take out trash and mow anyway. Don't waste your money on that stuff. Instead invest your money getting them to do something extraordinary!

For me, I deeply want my kids to read certain books that I pick out for them. Books like *The Case for Christ*, or *Fearless*, the story of Adam Brown. I pay my kids to read great books and discuss them with me, and I pay them for good grades on their report card and learning a musical instrument.

Whether it's exercising, reading or practicing an instrument, incentivize them financially to do things that will make them better men and women. Incentivize them to greatness, not to eat broccoli.[1]

My parents saw something in him and tilled the soil to cultivate the dream that would later become a reality. They motivated him to become a fearless leader, full of faith. And they enjoyed him. Three words stand out to me about our sons and how we, too, can grow them in their own dreams:

Cultivate

Motivate

Celebrate

Has the watchful eye of your parenting spied something in your son that you find unique or visionary? Do you see a great dream?

Cultivate it. Do you envision a successful man with God-given skills that you could influence with your values? Motivate it. Can you relax and cease stress and worry as you watch God work in the unique life of your boy? Celebrate it!

One day, Taylor disappeared to the garage. I had not noticed, yet it seems this had happened on occasion. I had not considered the smell of a baseball bat bag either—that is, until I heard Taylor's description of it. Then I could almost smell it myself. He described the smell of the leather glove and the sea salt on the sunflower seeds that scattered and lay on the bottom of the bag. The dirt on his cleats smelled of the finely raked field and the mound from which he pitched. His nose knowingly discerned the scent of the half-empty Gatorade bottles sure to be discarded. "Sometimes I go into the garage and just smell my bat bag," he said. My eyes widened and almost moistened as I heard the declaration of the seriousness of his dream. It was almost tangible, this passion for a game, and if he were to be successful, he would surely need a passion like this one. We decided a little more that day, in not-so-similar words, that we would cultivate this young man's dream; we would help it to grow and become a reality. We would motivate him to take risks and be confident and communicate exactly what he wanted to say, and we would celebrate. We would go and buy the ticket and wear the team merchandise and do whatever we needed to do to help our boy succeed in the unique way that God made him.

Not every boy is wild and crazy. I had lunch with a friend of mine last week, and we talked about our sons. Her son was what she called "highly sensitive" when he was little. Loud noises scared him. He did not like crowds of people. His socks bothered him. (We laughed about our boys having to have specific socks or cutting the seams out of their socks!) She told me that she read a book entitled *The Highly Sensitive Child* by Elaine N. Aron, PhD, and it was incredibly helpful: "Highly sensitive individuals are those born with a tendency to notice more in their environment and deeply reflect on everything before acting, as compared to those who notice less and act quickly and impulsively."[2] Aron's book contains lists of very specific things to do in specific situations. There is a huge difference between weak and calm. Your son may be quiet. He may be highly sensitive, or he may be an introvert, but still his heart is fierce.

It may not smell like leather or sunflower seeds, but your boy has a passion and a God-given talent. If he cannot smell it, maybe you can. Cultivate this giftedness in your son, whatever his God-given giftedness looks like, and motivate him to use everything he has to succeed. Celebrate what makes him unique and watch his beautiful story unfold.

> *For I know the plans I have for you, declares the Lord, plans to prosper you and not to harm you, plans to give you a hope and a future. (Jeremiah 29:11)*

When my son, Joelan, was twelve years old, I had a conversation with him after church one day, urging him to reach out to new kids his age that were coming and include them in his friend group. He looked at me and said, "Mom, I am not a leader. Don't make me a leader." I realized that day that I needed to back off and not put any pressure on him to be something he was not. Ten years later, while on a family mission trip to Honduras, I asked Joelan if he remembered that conversation. He told me he did not. Then he shared a statement that I will remember the rest of my life. He said, "Mom, you didn't have to make me a leader. God did that." The incredible life lesson I learned was that I needed to give up control and trust God to do his part in making my son the man he wanted him to be.

—Jennifer Howes

CHAPTER TWENTY-NINE

Honey, Your Son Has Testosterone

(Partnering in the battle against pornography.)

THE MAIL CAME EACH DAY AFTER LUNCH, AND I, NOT BEING UNAWARE, made it my job to sort through the posted articles in our box and differentiate between the necessary and good mail and the junk mail. I love to throw stuff away, as clutter has never been my friend. There was an annual mailing, however, that seemed to ignite my sorting energy in a most profound and purposeful way. I, having run cross-country in high school, reengineered my fast-paced skills as I spied the annual mailing. Each and every year, *Sports Illustrated* published their swimsuit edition and mailed it to all subscribers. I can assume eager patrons anticipated the edition. I, too, looked forward to being the first to grab the publication from the mailbox. My goal, however, was to dispose of the edition. Now, I am very much aware that swimsuits on beautiful models are not the worst thing. It is natural that men of all ages can appreciate God's creation. For heaven's sake, they are not naked, and it is a part of our culture to celebrate the body as a form of art, right? When my boys saw women in swimsuits and swam with their own friends in bikinis, why would I be such a guard dog over these pictures? I did not make a big deal about it. I did not scold or scoff. Brian and I decided years ago that we would be protectors of what came into our house, and this was one decisive way that we chose what pictures lay on our counters and our tables and filtered into the minds of our young boys. Brian and the boys knew that I "caught" the swimsuit editions and tossed them. I stated it once and they agreed. We never talked about it again.

I have been a filterer of more than the swimsuit edition. I toss department store sale papers with underwear models and ladies' magazines with sultry and scantily dressed women and girls. I purposefully do not subscribe to Victoria's Secret, as I can purchase my own undergarments without lingerie models on paper in my house. It is not because I am unaware. It is because I am aware. I am aware that the struggle is real for even good men who seek to follow after God. Men who are trying to do what is right are bombarded with pop-ups on their computers and billboards and commercials in stores, on the roads, and on TV. As a guardian of my home, I will quietly try to make a safe place where even soft pornographic material is not available or naively celebrated.

If you have not considered that your son has the potential to be tempted and affected by pornography or you do not realize that your husband has the potential to struggle with pornography, then you need to understand that men have been created with God-given testosterone. It is real and it is good, but the enemy wants to take what God made to be good and use it to shame and destroy.

One of my sweet friends was married in the fall of 1997. My son was her two-year-old ring bearer. As we were preparing for the wedding in the bridal room, the bridesmaids, the flower girl, and the ring bearer were readying to walk down the aisle. At the last minute, the bride needed to use the restroom, and being that her lovely wedding gown was so cumbersome, her helpful maids aided her in removing it. She was left with the lacy undergarments of a bride, adorned on her wedding day, which meant nothing to all of us females in the dressing room. There was, however, one very young unnoticed male in the bride's room: my two-year-old ring bearer, not much more than a baby, dressed in his tiny tux. As I sought to distract him from the undressing in the compact room, his eyes widened and he turned around as though he were a grown man. "I have never seen anything like that before!" he proclaimed. We burst into laughter, surprised at the honest comment. Right there, I realized that our little boys are miniature men with testosterone. I decided that day that I would never be ignorant, but I would partner with them against the little seemingly harmless things that could potentially become a snare.

I want to share some alarming statistics with you that are drawn from a research survey of studies on adolescents and pornography over the last twenty years:

- In 1995, 83 percent of boys and 48 percent of girls had viewed pornography online. Thirty percent of boys (10 percent of girls) viewed at least once a month. Keep in mind that in 1995, people barely knew how to create web pages.
- In 2005, 34 percent of adolescents had unwanted exposure to internet pornography.
- In 2011, 95 percent of boys and 50 percent of girls had ever viewed pornography.
- In 2011, 19 percent of adolescents had viewed violent pornography.
- In 2012, 44 percent of adolescents had consumed explicit sexual material online.
- In 2014, 52 percent of adolescents had watched pornographic movies or read pornographic magazines.[1]

The British Board of Film Classification was created in the UK to tackle the ease with which young people are exposed to pornography. According to their analysis, half of all eleven- to thirteen-year-olds have reported exposure, and "7 in 10 15- to 16-year-olds in the UK have seen pornography online." This early exposure to sexually explicit material often leads teenagers into habitual or purposeful searching for porn.[2]

Many years ago, our boys found themselves exposed to pornography in the locker rooms in middle school, as several of their classmates had porn on their phones. Similarly, I remember going to a new construction house and walking around the partially built home. As we walked from room to room and looked at the architecture, one of my boys found nude pictures in the unfinished bathroom drawer. Once, a pornographic magazine was lying on the ground in the church office parking lot! If you are not incredibly technological, you may not know that pictures on Instagram pop up that have been "liked" by the people you follow. Once, Zach restarted his whole Instagram with many fewer followers in order to eliminate the inappropriate pictures that were "liked" by some of his acquaintances in high school.

I share these things with you so that you might be informed and so that you may be called to action in defense of your son and his future healthiness as a man with a family. There are things that are beyond our control, but seek to do the things that you can control and let God handle the rest.

Brian and our boys have all three not only agreed but requested that Covenant Eyes be put on their phones and computers. Covenant Eyes is an app that blocks porn and questionable downloads and sends an email report of screen images. This accountability has been an encouragement for my grown-up boys, who want to fight against all the pulls of pornography that would seek to diminish their future marriage relationships and destroy their families. I want to encourage you to check it out. Find something that works for your family, and set up healthy parameters.

We do not need to be mail nazis. We do not need to shame or tease or be ignorant, but we want to be prayerful, educated parents who are wise and who set up our strong boys for success. Though widely accepted, pornography will shame and mock and disguise what is real and beautiful and diminish the passion that God created for a man to have with his own wife. It will confuse, numb, and belittle. Your son deserves for you to fight for him and with him in this battle. We do that in prayer and with wisdom and always with grace.

> *My son, keep my words, and store up my commands within you. Keep my commands and you will live, guard my teachings as the apple of your eye. Bind them on your fingers; write them on the tablet of your heart. Say to wisdom, "You are my sister," and to insight, "You are my relative." They will keep you from the adulterous woman, from the wayward woman with her seductive words. (Proverbs 7:1–5)*

Being the grandmother to three boys has been one of the greatest joys of my life. When watching from a grandparent's perspective, you recognize how quickly time flies. That's why we as grandmothers must invest in this next generation of young men. Many women may not feel like they have much to offer in shaping rambunctious little boys. But the opposite is true. There are three significant impacts a grandmother can have on her boys. First, champion their creativity. This allows them to see the endless possibilities of how God can use them to impact the world. Second, model unconditional love. Boys will be boys. They will break, stain, and rip things. Remember, they are more valuable than your valuables. Broken items or unintentional spills are opportunities for us to show the unconditional love of Jesus. Third, create fun environments. Boys like to be active, run, jump, move, laugh, and play. So make your home a place they enjoy and can be themselves. I have played Nerf gun war and spy adventures and made more forts that you could count. I've done all this in the name of bonding with my boys. Our boys value fun, and if I want to connect, I have to respect what they value. And when I appreciate what they value, they will grow up respecting my values.

—Cindy Lake, a.k.a. CiCi

CHAPTER THIRTY

Not Works. Grace

(Talking to your son about God and talking to God about your son.)

I CRIED AT THE AIRPORT YESTERDAY. IT IS NOT THAT I DID NOT WANT Taylor to fly to Australia to play winter baseball. I was not even remotely upset that he was going to be on the other side of the world on Christmas Day. We have been so ready for things to work out for him, and things have been so stressful that I was just thrilled that he was actually going.

I remember sitting in the bleachers his senior year of college and watching him break his hand in the game. It was broken in a very strategic and specific place that made him absolutely unable to pitch or hit. We found out the next day that if he had played one more game, his college career would have been over. However, his coach petitioned the NCAA and was able to give him a second senior year to come back and play. This was a very unlikely situation and required a note from a doctor and paper work. The puzzling thing for us was that as the players had been warming up during that game, Brian had decided to prayer walk the perimeter of the baseball field. He had been praying that God would do something that only he could do to help Taylor fulfill this dream to continue playing. The team was playing well, but neither the team nor Taylor was putting up eye-catching numbers, and a baseball future did not look promising.

When you ask God to help your son, you do not anticipate that your son will break his hand. Was that an answer to prayer? What was going on here? When we realized that he would be granted another year to play, we were overwhelmed and grateful.

That next season, several scouts came up the mountain to watch Taylor pitch and his cousin Caleb hit. It was fun to watch those two boys play the game they loved, now both seniors. Not far into the season, Taylor's shoulder began to hurt so badly that he could hardly lift his arm, let alone pitch. On occasion, he would drive an hour and forty-five minutes home after class to be prayed for by our friend Spencer, and then he would drive back for his afternoon class.

I remember hearing about him lying in the bullpen, unable to throw, praying that God would give him the ability to pitch in front of the scout that had just driven to the field to watch him. We were in a traffic jam that day and could not make it in time to see him pitch the best and fastest he ever had. I guess being alone in that dugout was what he needed. Taylor and God without Mom and Dad.

As his final college season ended and the professional baseball draft started, we found out that his name was actually on the board in the draft room, but that very morning, he got a call from a sports doctor confirming that his labrum was torn, and he would need surgery. We cried. Why? If God had been doing what only he could do in unbelievable ways, why was he going to let it end like this on this very day of the draft? I will admit that I have been mad at God many times about his handling of my sons' hearts. Have you?

Like the man of integrity that he is, he called the scout and the coach and told them that he was injured and would require surgery. He wanted to be honest with them, although they would never have known otherwise. The doctor even recommended that he not divulge that he was injured, in hopes of getting signed. But Taylor chose the high road—the long, lonely road—and was honest. The long story short is that he had a misdiagnosis and just had inflammation. Through physical therapy, he was ready to play again.

He received a call from a team in California when we were on a mission trip to Scotland. Again, Taylor and God had to figure this out. He flew to California and made the team. Each year since, we have had story after story of injury after injury and crazy ups and downs of emotion: "You are going to get to go and play. No, wait you are not. You are injured. No, wait. You are going to be OK. Maybe." We are learning that God is doing a work, as he does what only he can do at what seems to be the very, very last minute.

So I cried at the airport because, yet again, it seemed a no-go after months of work and anticipation. When the attendant said he could not fly, we knew he had the proper paper work from Australia. It seemed she had the power, though, to keep him from going. So I began to pray and texted everyone in the family to pray. I could almost tangibly feel the battle that was so familiar to his story. I watched as he got on his knees by the desk. He was not drawing any attention to himself, yet I knew he was praying for God to do something, something that again was out of our control. I was staying back and letting Brian work his kindness, knowing that Taylor was close to missing his flight. The whole family prayed, and our friends prayed, and I had a moment that was not about Taylor. It was about me. Could I trust God or not? Was God faithful or not? Even if things did not work out as we hoped, would I have faith that God was doing the best thing? It came down to me growing in my confidence in God amid my lack of control as I kept the tears inside my eyes. (Do you remember the father in the Bible who says, "I believe. Help my unbelief"? I think that was me.) I remembered that God had proven trustworthy, and whatever happened, it would be OK.

The Delta attendant at the next counter began talking out loud about God and very pointedly speaking about Jesus to the customer she was working with. Brian quickly spoke to her in a humorous yet desperate way and said that we needed some of that because we were praying that our son's paper work would go through. I promise you, she walked over and started praying in the name of Jesus. "This young man has all of his papers, and he needs to play baseball in Australia," she pleaded. "In the name of Jesus, I ask you to let this computer show he is approved!" Thirty seconds later, the screen changed, and Taylor was on his way to Australia! I watched from a distance as the attendant placed his suitcase on the scale and tagged it.

Do you ever feel like you are at the end of your emotional rope when it comes to your sons? That is usually when God shows himself to be powerful and attentive to the details we worry about. The Delta Air Lines lady knew so. Perhaps the most powerful way to teach your son about God is through his own life circumstances. Taylor knew that we could not fix his problems, but he knows that God did. It is exhausting, but I think it is worth it, right?

In Deuteronomy 11:19, God is talking to Israel and instructing them to pass his words on to their children: "So commit yourselves wholeheartedly to these words of mine. Tie them to your hands and wear them on your forehead as reminders. Teach them to your children. Talk about them when you are at home and when you are on the road, when you are going to bed and when you are getting up. Write them on the doorposts of your house and on your gates, so that as long as the sky remains above the earth, you and your children may flourish in the land the Lord swore to give your ancestors."

We cannot rely on the Delta ladies to teach our sons about God. Sure, these outside experiences contribute to some pretty cool faith stories and show us that God can do whatever he wants to do whenever he wants to do it. It is our job, however, to teach our boys about God and his Word. Not unlike every other parenting priority, we must be intentional about it. I want to encourage you to pick stories from the Bible and read them to your sons. Teach them the difference between real and make-believe. God's Word is real and true.

There are several things that our boys need to know about Jesus. He is God's Son; he is deity. That means that he too is God. He died on a cross for us and rose from the dead, and he is our only way to heaven. We could never be good enough to get to heaven. It is not about what we could do; rather, heaven is a free gift because of what Jesus did for us on the cross. Not works. Grace.

Whether your son hears about God from a *Veggie Tales* video as a little guy or you text him a verse that connects God's character with the challenges he faces as a young adult, it is your honor and responsibility as a parent to point your boy to truth and to God. He will be there for them when we cannot be there.

Not only must we talk to our sons about God, but we must talk to God about our sons. I am going to guess that you do that in some way. Perhaps, like me, you run out of things to pray. I can get in a shallow rut of praying so generally that I may not even know if God answered my prayers or not. I love what Mark Batterson says in *Draw the Circle: The 40-Day Prayer Challenge*: "God won't answer 100 percent of the prayers we don't pray. . . . Why do we mistakenly think that God is offended by our prayers for the impossible? . . . It's the impossible prayers that honor God because they reveal our faith and allow God to reveal His glory."[1] Batterson continues to talk about praying big prayers and challenges us with this: "Maybe our normal is so subnormal that normal seems abnormal. Maybe we need a new normal. Bold prayers and big dreams are normal . . . crazy miracles are the offspring of crazy faith. Normal begets normal. Crazy begets crazy. If we want to see God do crazy miracles [and I add 'crazy miracles for our boys'], sometimes we need to pray crazy prayers."[2]

Here are some very specific things that I pray for my boys. You may borrow my list or make your own list. Our bold prayers will directly affect our sons; even when they do not know how to pray for themselves, we can stand in the gap for them:

- Pray that your son will know God and that his heart would be bent toward God.
- Pray that your son will love the church and God's people.
- Pray that he will read God's Word and that it will keep him from sin.
- Pray that God would keep evil away from him.
- Pray that God would increase his influence and make him prosper.
- Pray for a breakthrough in specific areas of his life.
- Pray against generational sin and sickness.
- Pray for emotional, mental, and relational health.
- Pray for your son's wife and children even if they are not yet born.
- Pray that your whole line of future generations would come to know Jesus.
- Pray that he would see things that he cannot see and that God would open his eyes to the things he needs to become aware of.
- Pray for favor in the workplace and in the community.
- Pray that God will draw your son to himself as only he can do.
- Pray that he will be a strong leader and love his wife.
- Pray for peace in his home.
- Pray that your family will always be close.
- Pray that God would give your son great friendships and good influences.
- Pray that God would make him successful and that he will love what he does.
- Pray that God will give him joy and fulfillment that only he can bring.
- Pray that he would truly experience the love of God.
- Ask your son how you can pray for him.

Sometimes we need to speak boldly to our sons, and sometimes we pray boldly for years and wait to see what God will do. Zach has a degree in exercise science and a certification as a personal trainer. He loves the gym, and he always loved playing sports until his back injury in tenth grade, which kept him from continuing to play. College was a great experience for him, and he was able to play on several intermural teams. Zach decided last year that he was going to go to graduate school and get his master's degree. He later decided to specifically get that degree in seminary. Now, for many years we have prayed for God to point Zach in the direction that he wanted him to go and to make him successful in whatever he chose to do.

Zach has not known what he wanted to pursue, but he just felt like seminary was his next move. A few weeks ago, he joined Brian at an event that we hosted at our church. It was an event for ministry leaders, so Brian thought it might be beneficial. (And they were serving a great lunch!) So Zach showed up and sat attentively, not expecting that he would feel like the speaker was speaking directly to him. After the morning was over, he went to the speaker and asked him questions and shared a little bit about his story.

The message had been about giving God a full yes and not a half yes. Somehow this spoke directly to where Zach was and moved him to make a big decision that day. Zach decided that he needed to give a yes even though he did not know all the details or how things would work out for him. He knew that God was calling him to be a pastor. My boy said yes, and I was not there. I was just thrilled to hear the great news when he got home! I am so proud of him. I have seen for many years that he is at his best when he is serving people. I was just waiting and praying for him and God to sort it all out.

Sometimes you may not be there when God shows up and does something in the life of your boy, but your investments through the years will pay off. Your investment in teaching God's Word to your son and your investment in praying big, audacious prayers for him will impact him directly, for God is crazy about your boy! He loves him and is very interested in the details of his life. When you are not there, your son will remember what you taught him, and the investment of your prayers will continue to guide him.

> *And the Holy Spirit helps us in our weakness. For example, we don't know what God wants us to pray for. But the Holy Spirit prays for us with groanings that cannot be expressed in words. And the Father who knows all hearts knows what the Spirit is saying, for the Spirit pleads for us believers in harmony with God's own will. (Romans 8:26–27)*

I feel like the only thing I've ever done right as a mom is pray. I pray to God the Father, because he has already ordained every day of my son's life, and he's the only one who can change it. I pray to Jesus and ask him to whisper my son's name in his Father's ear every day, since he sits right beside him. And I pray to the Holy Spirit and ask him to show me what to pray and to pray the big-God-adventure things that I might not have the courage to hope for my son.

—Christy Murphy

CHAPTER THIRTY-ONE

How to Talk to Your Son about Racism

(You are seen.)

ONE NIGHT, WHEN I WAS STRUGGLING WITH MY TWO BOYS, WHO HAVE very different personalities, all three of us sat in a heap on the bathroom floor. One boy was crying and the other, nonemotional. I had attempted to use my counseling skills to help Taylor and Zach hear each other. I thought if they could voice their feelings and hear the feelings of the other that their inward desire for peace and their genuineness might prevail.

"What do you need from him?" I asked my broken son. He thought a minute and spoke through his sobs. "I need a hug." I turned to my other hurting son, misunderstood and bearing the pain of the emotions he held deeply within himself. "Are you serious? He wants a hug?" he responded. "That is what he said," I calmly pointed out. "You are kidding me," he retorted. I replied, "He is different from you, and he is obviously sitting here sobbing, and if he told you that he needs a hug, then you should probably get over here and hug him." My nerves were like frayed threads at this point, so I may not have said all the right things. I bet you have been there.

What happened next was a breakthrough moment. In a reluctant but honest move forward, my boy hugged his hurting brother and received a gripping, weeping, needed embrace that seemed to exude a healing effect that even I could feel at a distance. His brother's moist eyes were closed tightly as he was being held by the brother that hurt him. He soaked in the love; even though it was not an original idea, it felt authentic enough and it soothed.

Friends, our country is full of brothers who have been carrying hurt for generations. In no way am I suggesting that a hug is enough to bring healing and understanding in every situation. However, empathy and acknowledgment are great first steps in understanding how a brother authentically feels, given his lived experience. A brother who has been hurt desires to be heard, seen, understood, and ultimately embraced. The brother that has either caused the hurt, benefitted from the hurt, or turned a blind eye to the hurt must take an honest self-assessment and come alongside his brother to correct the wrong. In this chapter, I am going to address something that I know very little about. I do not in any way see myself as an expert on racism. I do, however, see a need to have this conversation and to help people move in a direction of healthiness, as our country is in a most tumultuous state and my friends have heavy hearts.

I Never Prayed like Her

There are many and various restaurant options in the Atlanta area, and with so many places to choose from, we tried a new, delicious BBQ restaurant with our friends, Patrick and Lynnette. Pat is an accountant, and Lynnette is a business professional in the greater Atlanta area. We were delighted to get to know them on a more personal level, as Pat was a new member of the leadership team at our church. Their two little boys reminded me of having two little boys the same number of years apart, and so we laughed and talked about the joys and challenges of parenting boys. Everything Lynnette said was familiar to me. I had walked the same path. We compared stories of her boys and my older boys, and human nature's tales drew us together through the bonds of nurturing. However, our conversation brought about a crossroads of understanding, and I found myself completely unaware and devoid of the ability to relate.

As Lynnette referred to the recent news of the horrific deaths of Black men around our country, she shared with me that she was afraid. Why was she scared? I leaned in. "I pray for the safety of my little Black boys," she said with concern. That had never crossed my mind. I pray a lot of things for my boys, but because they are White, I had not comprehended personally how my friend felt, especially with the recent deaths of boys who were brown. We went on to talk more about that. I now realize that there are things that I never had to consider that keep other mothers on their knees with heavy hearts. Patrick and Lynnette and so many others have been gracious and vulnerable to share their reality with us. They have allowed us to ask ignorant questions and have walked with us as we have continued to gain understanding.

My Misunderstanding and the Truth of the Matter

Now, I want to be very transparent and tell you what I have thought for decades. Forgive me because I just did not know. Maybe this will help you if you are a reader with a similar background. I grew up in predominately White neighborhoods in North Carolina. We moved to northern Indiana and to South Florida during my years growing up. We were a Christian family who always sought to love God and people. We were the type of people to get along with anyone, no matter their background or ethnicity. Aside from one relative, I largely did not know any White people who did not like Black people. I honestly did not understand what the problem was. I understood that slavery was a horrific thing, but it was over, right? And we were all equal, right? I assumed that if my Black friends "appeared" to be OK, then everything was OK. Our cultures are different, sure, but isn't that what makes mankind beautiful? I thought we all had the same opportunities if we all worked hard. However, despite what I believed nestled in the insulation of my own life, the world around me was telling me otherwise; racial division, social injustice, and racism were real.

I now see that God has been bringing me through baby steps of understanding, and if you are White, this is what you need to understand. Racism reveals itself not only through the conscious intolerance of people of other races but through a system of social advantage based on race. A structure of social hierarchy continues to persist, supported by cultural messages, misuse of power, and institutional bias. Many Black people have not had the same opportunities that many White people have had, and they themselves, and not just their great-grandparents, have experienced racism. They have been talking about it, but the nation, for the most part, has not been listening. Many have experienced bitterness and a lack of trust. Some feel like they must just survive. It's scary, and they are exhausted from walking what seems like an uphill journey when possibly our journey has been on flat ground and we just did not know it, for they have been walking on a slope their whole lives.

I have asked my friend Cecilia Lester, who cofounded Love Beyond Walls, an Atlanta-based organization that brings hope and dignity to those experiencing homelessness, to share her honest thoughts on talking to her son about racism. Here is what she said:

> There have been moments as a mother where I have feared for the life of my young ten-year-old son. I never imagined when he got older that I would have to let him know that when he became a certain age, he would no longer be

considered cute but rather a threat to someone. We as Black mothers have to have "the talk" with our sons about certain situations. If and when they encounter a cop, not to run or make any sudden moves. They would also need to keep their hands in plain view and not reach for anything in their pockets. African American mothers advise their sons not to do pranks to people of other races, since that can be a threat because of their race. This can help them avoid racism. If my son is walking down the street, I would caution him to not wear a hoodie over his face where people can't see his eyes. This is what Trayvon Martin was doing, and it ultimately ended in his untimely death. Color blindness affects people, making them unable to view color in the normal way. I have had to tell my son that he has to be careful when dating girls outside of his race, as it is important to make sure to meet their families because there could be a history of their family not wanting their daughter to date outside of their race. We don't think that way, but not everyone is like our family.

As mothers, our hearts are connected even when our skin colors are different. What should we do to help, and how can we inform our boys? We need to be aware, to be willing to listen and ask questions and hug the brother who is sobbing. We can teach our sons that God created everyone equally, and we can model to them the importance of embracing others who do not necessarily look like them. May we and our boys be able to sustain healthy conversations as we grow in understanding. It may take time for our nation to heal, but with understanding and a lot of willingness to love and listen, we can be a little part of shaping the next generation to hear others and help them know that they are seen.

> *So in Christ Jesus you are all children of God through faith. (Galatians 3:26)*

As mothers, our children are our primary disciples. It is our job to interpret the world for them. It is also our honor to help them feel safe enough to be who God created them to be, as the world will be pressing in on them on all sides to conform in one way or another. I believe it is paramount to ensure that my sons have time to just be boys while they are young—they will have the rest of their lives to be men. As they are becoming men, it is not lost on me that they will see me as their first and primary example of what a woman, wife, mom, leader, engineer, and theologian are; they are growing up with sisters and the normalization that women are equal and capable people, partners, and friends. I believe this is my greatest service—our greatest service—to our sons . . . to present ourselves wholly rather than compartmentally in our discipleship of them.

—Veronica Gravely, engineer

Our seven- and nine-year-old boys are filled with curiosity, innocence, adventure, and unconditional love. I often selfishly wish that I could freeze them in time or hit the snooze button a few more minutes before I must awaken them to the realities of people of color in this world. I know shielding and isolating them is not the answer. As an African American mom, I am compelled to prepare the boys at home to love God and love others, believe in themselves, know their self-worth, use their voice to help others, understand their cultural history beyond slavery, and treat others with dignity and respect no matter what their ethnicity. Currently, I sleep well knowing the boys are across the hall fast asleep with their legs dangling over the bunk bed railing. But one day they will be teenagers or grown men even, and I often wonder if someone will mistreat or misjudge them simply because of their brown skin. Will the boys make it home safely from a routine trip to the store? Daily, I petition the Lord on their behalf, not knowing what the future holds but trusting the One (Christ) who holds their future. I seize every moment to help guide Josiah and Matthew in a way that makes this world a better place. I recall this one occasion when my oldest son (who was seven years old at the time) and I were coming out of the library and he noticed workers painting the building. He said, "Mommy, why do I always see that group of people painting?" I said, "Son, painting is just one of the many jobs that they do; they are also doctors, lawyers, teachers, chefs, and a host of other occupations." You see, I am not just preparing our boys to face racism, but we are raising them to dispel stereotypes and to be antiracist.

—Lynnette Reid

CHAPTER THIRTY-TWO

Girls Are Different

(Treat them like queens.)

MORGAN AND MAGGIE WANTED TO SHOP! AS THE AVENUE SUMMONED us with its array of lovely stores, I took my two nieces on a little shopping trip. They were staying with us for a few days while my sister and her husband went to a cabin in the mountains. The girls took bubble baths in my big bathtub and played basketball with the boys. They snuggled the dogs and made cookies. Today, however, was shopping day, and I was eager with anticipation, as I had not shopped with girls in forever. Let me commence by first sharing with you how my men shop. First, they see something they want, and second, they buy it. Done deal. They do not have a lot of feelings about it. The trip is short and productive. The mission, as it seems, is accomplished. and then they require a meal. It is fun, actually, as Brian usually is drawn to the exact outfit the mannequin is wearing. He purchases the best-looking thing in the store and then finds the closest Starbucks. Shopping with the guys is great. I almost always get what I want because the answer is always "Get it." Sometimes the answer is "Get it and let's go." Either way, I get it. And then I get Starbucks. Boy shopping. It is a trip.

What I did not perceive with my nieces is that somehow I had obliviously grown accustomed to boy shopping. I had left a small piece of my femininity behind, perhaps when I ruthlessly became so outnumbered. But that was all so long ago. On this day, we were girl shopping! First, we got ready to shop. We wanted to look our best as we browsed all the latest fashions, as this was an experience. We did our hair. We ironed our clothes, and we looked for the lost accessory that made the outfit make sense in the first place. We made a plan and talked about what we hoped to find and what we might purchase if we could not find our first choice. We shared what we thought might be a good look on each other, and we told stories of past successful purchases.

As we arrived and found a parking space, we first went to American Eagle. I was excited that my elementary– and middle school–aged nieces both liked the same store, and the fact that I liked it too, well, it was a win, and we were off to a great start. They tried on many outfits and modeled them for me and each other while taking pictures and deciding if each color was complimentary. They looked adorable, and the outfits they found were just what I call a ten! Girls were so fun! We were having a blast. "So, girls, which one did you decide on?" I inquired with anticipation. Their parents had left them a certain amount of money to spend on shopping, and they were going to purchase the best things the Avenue had to offer. I too had planned to help them buy something they loved and would wear to remember our girl shopping day. They would return home to their friends with those fun "out-of-town" clothes, looking desirably different yet blending in with their friends. It is a thing when you shop out of town. You wear something that no one else can match, and you look mysteriously fabulous. "We think we are going to try another store," the girls said. What? I was confused. I thought we all loved all the outfits, but OK, let's keep shopping!

We looked in another store and then another. These cuties donned jewelry and hats, and then we continued our search for whatever it was we were looking for. We took pictures and sent them to their mother. We went from one retailer to another as they scanned the racks and searched for sizes. After quite a while, I began to feel slightly tired, my feet began to ache, and I felt curiously hungry. Was I accustomed to the boy shopping meal that was to ensue shortly after the purchase? I was about to ask if the girls wanted to eat when one of them exclaimed, "I can't find anything, so let's just go back to the first store." Great! We were getting somewhere. The process of elimination was tried and true. They had explored all the possibilities. They had combed, dredged, and hunted, and now we were going to narrow down the prospects and make a purchase.

What happened next left me in a complete state of bewilderment. The girls decided that they would simply wait and not buy anything at all. What? I tried to wrap my conditioned mind around that fact. The shopping experience was wrought with great purpose and intention, and like a hunter who deliberately let his prey walk away, I was confused. Was everyone happy? Would I be required to endure more clothing possibilities if we did not bring home a prize? We bought some fancy pastries from a local bakery and moseyed back home to the boys.

I learned two things that day. Number one, my nieces are super-cool and even back then had such style. Number two, girls are very, very different from boys.

As I consider the contrast between boys and girls, my mind's eye sees my little brother with his head sticking out of the rear car window. Bless his heart. He had three big sisters who incessantly powdered and brushed and glossed in the car. He couldn't breathe with all the smells, he said. One man with four mothers. It is a wonder he made it out safely into the arms of the military.

I do regret that as a boy mom, I tried to be a little too accommodating and low maintenance. I honestly think I would have helped everyone in the long run if I had acted more girly. What I mean is that I chose to watch the sports movies and war movies with my guys and rarely if ever made everyone watch a chick flick. I did not really do a lot of girl nights with nail painting, and well, as I type this, maybe what I need now is a long-overdue beach trip with the girls!

Here are a few things that our boys need to know about girls in general, especially if they do not have a sister:

It is normal for girls to cry. It is not normal for them to cry all the time or to be manipulative, but crying is OK. I was not a big crier, but I do wish I could go back and expose a few more of the tears I shed in the back room to educate my sons about the normalcies of women.

Girls generally take longer to get ready to go somewhere. Literally, I would make an announcement and the boys would grab their hats and tennis shoes and get in the car. You cannot expect girls to be ready in five minutes. Patience will go a long, long way in their futures as they learn to be stress-free, as they may have to wait on their lovely ladies, much like Andy Griffith in the song "Waitin' on a Woman" by Brad Paisley.

Women are responders, and so are girls. If a boy treats a girl with respect and honor, he will usually get a positive response. If he deposits guilt or shame or distrust, he will reap a whirlwind in response. If a woman withdraws emotionally, he should look at the fact that she is most likely responding to his actions.

Women often have an intuition or an instinct about people's character. Men would do well to listen to their wives' advice, and boys should be taught to appreciate that girls see things differently.

One of the greatest needs of women and girls is security.

Girls usually have a nesting, nurturing instinct.
Dr. James Dobson, in his book *Bringing Up Boys*, referred
to observing the innate differences in the way girls and
boys played with only a stick. Most of the boys used it as a
weapon, and many of the girls wrapped it in a blanket and
rocked it like a baby. Girls are made to love and cherish.

Girls may change their minds several times. It's sort of
a thing, and it is OK.

Beauty habits cost money. It may take more money than
boys think to support the beauty habits of a girly girl. The
costs of hair color, nail salons, makeup, skincare, waxing,
and accessories are shocking to learn if a boy has never
had a sister. When girls feel good about themselves, they
seem to be more confident. No one wants a spoiled girl, as
there needs to be a balance there, but you do not want to
withhold those things that make a woman feel beautiful
or you will have a woman who does not feel beautiful, and
that is not a good thing.

**Girls run in packs and generally tell their friends
everything.** I remember sitting at a chicken restaurant
with our boys when one of them started texting a girl.
There was some secret information involved, and this
young lady seemed to be trying to pry this information
from my middle school–aged son. I, knowing about girls
because I am one, suggested that this young lady was most
likely with her friends that very moment and was sharing
the whole conversation with them. All three of my men
doubted me and laughed at my suggestion, but in the end,
I was right. The girls were all together at a friend's house
following the whole text thread. Yes, ma'am, girls do talk.

Sometimes girls at school can be mean to each other.

Girls have a question in their heart. I mentioned in my chapter "Jumbo Ketchup Bottles" that men and boys have a God-given question: "Do I have what it takes?" Similarly, every woman and little girl has a question. Stasi Eldredge addresses this in her book *Captivating*—which I highly recommend, by the way. Each little girl and every old lady has the same question: "Am I lovely?" Although we can only look to God ultimately to answer our question, it is the honor and responsibility of men to answer the question for their wives and little girls with a resounding "Yes, you are lovely indeed!"[1]

Girls love beauty because God loves beauty, and girls are created in his image. Do not shame them for that. The desire of a girl to be lovely is a reflection of her heavenly Father, and the beauty of nature is her gift.

Sometimes, when girls are emotional, they do not want boys to fix all their problems. They may just need them to listen attentively. Respond to their hearts and emotions first, and then when you have tackled that, they will be able to listen, and you can work on the solutions together.

Girls may get their feelings hurt more easily. It would be nice if women came with a manual, but we do not. It is important for men and boys to understand that if they do, by chance, figure out the manual of a woman's mind, it will most certainly continue to change as she grows older!

Sheri Rose Shepherd states in her book *Preparing Him for the Other Woman*, "It's as if husbands grew up going to Man School. They have no trouble passing the 'guy' courses: Acting Cool 101, Success and Achievement 102, and Sports 400. All of the skills learned in those classes come naturally and are only reinforced through peer pressure. On the other hand, while men often pass Getting the Girl 101, most guys flunk out of Understanding Women 101. Why? Because no one teaches this course in the school of married life!"[2]

As parents, it is our responsibility to train our little boys and our big boys to respect girls. If we can impart to them these simple truths and give them a desire to understand the most important ladies in their lives, we will have given them a gift that will forever impact their future healthiness and the emotionally healthy state of their future families.

> *So the Lord God caused the man to fall into a deep sleep. While the man slept, the Lord God took out one of the man's ribs and closed up the opening. Then the Lord God made a woman from the rib, and he brought her to the man. "At last!" the man exclaimed. "This one is bone from my bone and flesh from my flesh! She will be called woman because she was taken from man." (Genesis 2:22–23 NLT)*

In my son's years of imaginary play, his costume rotation consisted of a police officer, firefighter, and soldier. He put the costume on and, in those roles, would get to work arresting us, holding a hose, or hiding behind a couch with a Nerf gun.

Even as a little boy, he knew he had an important job to do. And people in his life who would applaud him for it. Having a girl before having my boy, I needed to shift my approach to showing love. Instead of playing dollhouse, I pitched baseballs. Instead of "You look beautiful," I said, "Good job, buddy." Instead of painting fingernails, I let him wrestle me. The same love is shown in such dramatically different ways with boys and girls. And when that tiny little bundle of blue becomes a teenager, he will eat *everything*.

—Emily Morgan

CHAPTER THIRTY-THREE

Furby

(The end.)

IN 1998, TIGER ELECTRONICS RELEASED AN ELECTRONIC ROBOT ANIMAL toy that spoke and blinked and waved its arms. Furby was translated into twenty-four languages and in three short years was sold to forty million lucky little kids. He was a freaky creature, waving and responding to being talked to and fed. If you walked by Furby, his eyes might move toward you. If you spoke to him, he would respond. By the early turn of the century, Furby was still the rage, which meant that Brian's mom bought one for Taylor, and I tried not to look at it. It gave me the creeps.

I drove one afternoon to run errands with Taylor and little Zach, who was in a baby carrier, and Furby accompanied us in the van (the green van). It must have been a challenging parenting day because by the time I rounded the corner of Ridge Road, I had had enough. "Calm down now or Furby is going out the window," I threatened. The threat of losing Furby only accelerated Taylor's fit of rage, and as promised, I threw Furby out! As soon as I hurled him (Furby, that is) out the window, Taylor let out a shrill scream and wailed all the way home. The electronic animal landed in a puddle, his arms waving up and down as he called out in his native Furby language. I know this because I called Brian when I got home. "If you want the Furby that your mom bought Taylor, then you can go pick him up on the corner at Ridge Road. I had enough bad behavior and threw him out," I calmly admitted. "What?" Brian was not exactly happy that his mother's not-so-cheap gift had landed on the side of the road. Had his wife lost it? He brought Furby, still waving and talking, back to his office and cleaned him in the sink. I have never lived this story down.

Maybe I am not the only one who has lost it a time or two. There are no perfect parents. Just remember to be faithful in the little things and teach your boys to follow hard after Jesus. That is what really matters.

Pray as hard as you can on your knees for those little boys, because I promise you, God hears from heaven and is banking all those timeless prayers, and he will never forget one of them. When we seek God for our boys, we will see him open doors and clear out an amazing path, and we will look back and know that it was God who did it.

You will have a tendency to just be a mother and forget about your man. He will be really tired too, and you must put him first. We default to taking care of the demands of our boys, but your man will be there when everyone is grown up. Love him first.

Remember that God keeps all his promises. He has never ever failed, and he will never leave you or your precious boy. You can trust him.

You have everything you need to raise this boy!

You are incredibly loved.

> *I can do all things through Christ, who gives me strength. (Philippians 4:13)*

Discussion Guide

Chapter questions for group discussion:

1. **You're Gonna Miss This**
   A. What do you already miss about your son being little?
   B. What may be driving you crazy right now, but you have a feeling you will look back and miss it?
   C. Why is it important to focus on the grace we have been given for just this one day?

2. **Jumbo Ketchup Bottles**
   A. Why is it so important to understand the heart of a boy and to value the fierce soul that he has been given?
   B. In what ways have you unknowingly tried to tame your son's warrior spirit?
   C. What qualities or behaviors do you see in your young son that, given time, might turn into attributes of a great man?

3. **We Got an A on Our Gorilla Science Project**
   A. Can you recall a time when a parent or grandparent helped you out and instead of spoiling you, their kindness gave you hope and encouragement?
   B. Why do you think that parents often want to allow their boys to learn the hard way? Is this good or bad? Is there a balance?
   C. Is there a specific way that you can show love and bring hope to your son by helping him with something this week?

4. **I Should Have Been an Orthopedic Doctor!**
   A. Is your son calm or energetic? Did you expect him to be this way?
   B. How do you think we can best balance protecting our boys and keeping them safe with letting go, taking risks, and learning to trust?
   C. Have you or a family member had an injury that marked you in a powerful way? How has that affected the way that you parent?

5. **Spit It Out**
   A. Do you find that your choice of communication affects the way your son reacts to you? How is that?
   B. What do you observe about situations where preschool-age boys do not listen?
   C. How do you think speaking respectfully to a teen boy might influence his actions and reactions?

6. **I Left My Boy on Top of a Mountain**
   A. Can you recall a time when you heard your son repeat something that you had said, and you knew he had been listening to you?
   B. Explain the levels of faith that you must have to release your son to go his way after you have instructed him.
   C. What is the best way to react when your son does not heed your advice and you see him make mistakes?

7. **Buy Yourself a Pink Towel**
   A. What are the warning signs in your own life that may indicate that you are under a lot of stress and may tell you that you need to take a break and do something to take care of yourself?

B. What are the things that fill your emotional bucket?

C. Sometimes we take care of everyone else and we fail to care for ourselves, but in the long run, we will be able to care for others better if we prioritize our own emotional healthiness. What next step can you take to value self-care?

8. Cutting the Grass with Scissors

   A. What do you value or appreciate about the out-of-the-box thinking of someone you may know with ADD?

   B. How can you support parents and boys who are on a journey of managing ADD?

   C. If your son had ADD, would you want to know it? To what lengths would you go to make sure he had everything he needed to be successful? Do you need to take a step in that direction? What might your next step look like?

9. Fight Night

   A. Do you have any bad parenting stories?

   B. Have you looked at other parents and judged them because of the choices their boys make? Have you given credit to yourself because you have a "good boy"?

   C. How can we ultimately give God the credit when our boys make good choices and when we are seen as good parents?

10. Everything Is a Sword

   A. Do you ever hear frustrated mothers barking at their boys in the grocery store? How does that make you feel?

   B. Why do you think parents needlessly say no to so many things? How do you think saying yes to as much as possible can eventually have a positive impact on your son?

   C. What is one area where you are trying to say yes?

11. No Sceered Men
    A. What fears have you seen in little boys and grown men? How are those fears similar?
    B. What might your son attempt to accomplish if he were fearless?
    C. What are you currently doing that is teaching your son to be fearful? What step can you take personally to instill courage instead of fear into your son's heart?

12. Pierced and Tatted
    A. The key principles we instill may outweigh the benefits of the "good" behavior we try to gauge. Why are parents often more interested in measurable actions than they are in imprinting foundational values and beliefs?
    B. What is one core value that you have already begun to teach your son? How is this going to shape him in the future?
    C. What is one life-giving truth that you want to bestow on your son's foundational belief system? What next step are you taking to ensure that he gets it?

13. Dancing with a Dolphin
    A. What is one of the best family experiences you have had with your son? What made it so special?
    B. What is a happy and inexpensive family activity that you have stored in your memory from growing up?
    C. In our society, we tend to buy our boys more than we had when we were young. What do you need to do next to invest your time in a fun, memorable family experience with your son?

14. Green Van
    A. Can you remember an answered prayer from your childhood?

    B. Do you have any green van stories when God did something just because he could? How does that increase your faith that he just might do that again?

    C. What is a present need that you could share and pray for together as a family?

15. Don't Act Shocked

    A. Recall a time when your son told you something and you truly were shocked, but you reacted well and he felt like he could confide in you.

    B. Were you able to really share your thoughts with your own parents? If not, in whom did you feel you could confide? Why do you think this is?

    C. What is a one-line statement or question that you can have up your sleeve that you have prepared and thought through for shocking conversation moments?

16. Fire Pit Conversations

    A. In general, describe your family's style of doing things. Does your conversation about God and the Bible reflect the way you normally do things, or is it somewhat forced?

    B. Share a meaningful and relevant conversation you have had with your son about God.

    C. Have you ever prayed for a specific opportunity to share something on your mind or heart and God gave you an obvious opportunity? What happened?

17. Little Monsters That Drive People Insane

    A. How do you feel when you encounter a disrespectful, disobedient boy?

    B. Why do you think people choose to not train their boys?

    C. What are the benefits of purposefully training your son?

18. Heroes
    A. Was your dad a hero to you when you were growing up? Explain.
    B. Mothers have the unique ability to point out the hero qualities in dads. What admirable quality in your husband can you choose to acknowledge this week to your son?
    C. How do you see God as your heavenly Father?

19. Time to Paint!
    A. Why is it important to alternate energetic and calm activities when your boys are little?
    B. Sometimes mental exercise, giving our boys a challenge to solve, can be energizing and competitive. What puzzles, games, and activities do you find to be calming and exciting at the same time?
    C. How can you encourage your son to be physically active and enjoy the outdoors?

20. Dumb Men in Commercials
    A. Prayers for our men are vital. How can we pray for the men who influence our sons?
    B. Why is a strong male role model so important for a boy?
    C. Does your son have a father, grandfather, or male relative to look up to and learn from? If not, what could be your next step in connecting him with a coach, teacher, or mentor as a role model?

21. Sliding on the Bannister
    A. At some point, we learn the art of comparison and we measure ourselves and our worth as individuals against what other people think. We even compare our parenting to that of other parents. Why do we have the tendency to do this?

B. Have you ever been shamed for something your son did? How did that make you feel?

C. If you loved people fully yet did not look to them for approval, how much more freedom could you experience as a parent and as an individual?

22. Sometimes You Can't Fix It
    A. Can you think of a time when your faith was small, but God brought you through a difficult time? Do you see a string of God's faithfulness in your life?
    B. How do you feel when you cannot fix something that is broken in your son's life?
    C. How can you point your son to Jesus even when your faith is small?

23. Do I Know You?
    A. What were you like in middle school?
    B. Why do you think the middle school years are so daunting?
    C. In the spirit of majoring on the major things and letting go of the little things, share one example of a major thing that you will not compromise and one example of something that is not worth fighting over that you could currently let go.

24. You Are Basically a Taxi Driver
    A. In what season of life are you currently parenting? What do you like best about this season?
    B. What is something that you look forward to doing, but it is not your season to do it yet?
    C. How in the midst of your daily chaos can you choose to embrace your season?

25. I Did Spit on the Floor
    A. Have you had any less-than-graceful reactions to poor behavior?
    B. What positive, successful disciplinary action have you seen modeled?
    C. What does it look like for you to be consistent right now?

26. You Have Baggage
    A. Have you observed positive or even challenging attributes in your son that you see mirrored in yourself?
    B. If you knew that gaining an understanding of your own baggage would ultimately prevent a lot of difficulty for your son, would you be willing to take a closer look into your past?
    C. God has the ability to take all of our history and turn even our ashes into beauty. How is he making a beautiful story out of the imperfect parts of your life?

27. The First Five Minutes
    A. How do mothers set tones in their homes? Why is this so important to consider?
    B. What kind of tone setter do you want to be? Why?
    C. Preparing for the first five minutes of tone setting takes thought and intentionality. How might you coach yourself into being a positive tone setter?

28. My Brother, Camo, and Military History
    A. How are the men in your life (sons, brothers, father, husband, etc.) uniquely different from each other?
    B. How can you cultivate and motivate and celebrate your son in the unique way God made him?
    C. Are you a worrier? How can you best pray and then sit back and watch God create a beautiful story in your son's life?

29. Honey, Your Son Has Testosterone
    A. What is the difference between "trusting your son" and being aware of the pervasive pornography problem that is targeting our boys?
    B. Why do you think people avoid talking about pornography with their sons?
    C. How can we pray specifically against pornography and pray for our husbands and sons?

30. Not Works. Grace
    A. Describe a naturally occurring conversation you have had with your son about God.
    B. Why is it important to be specific and ask God for big things when we pray?
    C. Most people appreciate being prayed for. Would you consider asking your son how you can pray for him?

31. How to Talk to Your Son about Racism
    A. Have you become a listener to people who do not look like you? What have you heard that you did not expect to hear?
    B. Do most people think racism is a problem? Why or why not?
    C. How can you help your son to value people who do not look like him?

32. Girls Are Different
    A. How has being a boy mom changed you?
    B. What advice would you give your son about the way a girl would like to be treated?
    C. Girls are strong and equal, but they are different from boys. How can we teach our sons to be supportive and protective at the same time?

33. Furby

    A. Mothers often feel like they are not enough and they are not doing enough. Do you ever feel that way? Why?

    B. If you are married, how can you prioritize your relationship with your husband?

    C. What three or four specific things does God love about you?

Notes

Chapter Two: Jumbo Ketchup Bottles

1 James C. Dobson, *Bringing Up Boys: Practical Advice and Encouragement for Those Shaping the Next Generation of Men* (Carol Stream, IL: Tyndale Momentum, 2001).

Chapter Five: Spit It Out

1 Jen Hatmaker, *For the Love: Fighting for Grace in a World of Impossible Standards* (Nashville: Nelson Books, 2015), 81.

2 "20 Ways to Talk So Your Kids Will Listen," Child Development Institute, accessed July 21, 2021, https://childdevelopmentinfo.com/how-to-be-a-parent/communication/talk-to-kids-listen/#gs.73be29.

Chapter Eleven: No Sceered Men

1 Aditi Subramaniam, "The Neurobiology of Fear: How Much of Fear Is Inborn?," *Psychology Today*, October 3, 2019, https://www.psychologytoday.com/us/blog/parenting-neuroscience-perspective/201910/the-neurobiology-fear.

2 Zach Williams, "Fear Is a Liar," track 7 on *Chain Breaker*, Essential Records 083061105327, 2017, compact disc.

3 "What Does It Mean to Fear the Lord?," *Olive Tree Blog*, accessed June 21, 2021, https://www.olivetree.com/blog/what-does-it-mean-to-fear-the-lord/.

Chapter Thirteen: Dancing with a Dolphin

1 Karol Ladd, *The Power of a Positive Mom* (West Monroe, LA: Howard Books, 2001), 194.

2 Paul Faulkner, *Raising Faithful Kids in a Fast-Paced World* (West Monroe, LA: Howard Books, 1995), 295.

3 Faulkner, 297.

4 Ladd, *Power of a Positive Mom*, 193.

Chapter Seventeen:
Little Monsters That Drive People Insane

1 Faulkner, *Raising Faithful Kids*, 82.
2 Faulkner, 104–5.
3 Faulkner, 104.
4 Faulkner, 185–86.

Chapter Eighteen: Heroes

1 Faulkner, *Raising Faithful Kids*, 316–17.
2 Faulkner, 130, 148.

Chapter Nineteen: Time to Paint!

1 Serena B. Miller and Paul Stutzman, *More Than Happy: The Wisdom of Amish Parenting* (New York: Howard Books, 2015), 268.
2 Brad Lomenick, "Make Time for Margin," February 25, 2013, http://www.bradlomenick.com/brad-lomenick-3/make-time-for-margin.

Chapter Twenty: Dumb Men in Commercials

1 Glenn T. Stanton, "The Unique Matter of Manhood," Focus on the Family, November 11, 2017, https://www.focusonthefamily.com/manhood/the-unique-%E2%80%A8matter-of-%E2%80%A8manhood/.
2 Stanton.
3 Robert Lewis, *Raising a Modern-Day Knight* (Wheaton, IL: Tyndale House, 1997), 67.

Chapter Twenty-One: Sliding on the Bannister

1 Dr. Seuss, *Happy Birthday to You* (New York: Random House, 1959).

Chapter Twenty-Three: Do I Know You?

1 James Dobson, "Q & A: Tough Teens, Pt. 2," Dr. James Dobson Family Institute, July 14, 2021, https://www.drjamesdobson.org/mobile-items/q-tough-teens-pt-2.
2 Dobson.
3 Dobson.